MOUNTAIN MEN AND THE RENDEZVOUS

FUR TRAPPERS, EXPLORERS, TRADERS, SCOUTS
AND THEIR
ROWDY GATHERINGS

LIZ SARTORI

Wildrose Press

Garland, UT
wildrose.enterprises@gmail.com

Copyright © 2014 Liz Sartori

All rights reserved.

ISBN: 0990511359
ISBN-13: 978-0-9905113-5-9

DEDICATION

Al and Susanne Loris took me to my first rendezvous.

Jenny and Dale "Sasquatch" Cottrell welcomed me into their world and amazed me with their mountain man craftsmanship.

Frankie Reimschussel first encouraged me to write.

CONTENTS

1	History of the Fur Trade and Fur Trapping	1
2	Land Claims and Fur Companies	11
3	Forts in the Days of the Mountain Men	17
4	Food, Clothing and Shelter	23
5	How to Trap a Beaver in the Rocky Mountains	29
6	Peter Skene Ogden	33
7	Etienne Provost	39
8	Ceran St. Vrain	45
9	Bill Williams	51
10	Joe Walker	59
11	Hugh Glass	65
12	Jedediah Smith	71
13	Thomas Fitzpatrick	81
14	Kit Carson	91
15	Jim Baker	97
16	Jim Beckwourth	103
17	John Colter	109
18	Jim Bridger	113
19	Liver-eating Johnson	121
20	Modern-day Rendezvous	135

PREFACE

During the early 1800's, many young men, unhappy with city life in St. Louis or elsewhere, or escaping an indentured or apprenticed fate someone else had chosen for them, took to the wilds of the little-known, adventure-filled West and Northwest. From Canada to Taos, New Mexico, the Missouri River to the Pacific, the primitive life of the Indian coupled with the lucrative fur trade drew these Mountain Men into heart-pounding moments in the wilderness, interspersed with isolation and the ribald rendezvous.

ACKNOWLEDGMENTS

Thanks to Dale "Sasquatch" Cottrell for the mountain man artifacts throughout this book.

Thanks to Julie and Dan "Log-Killer" James, whose mountain man firearms grace this book.

Thanks to Ned A. Carter for going the extra mile with his tech support.

Special thanks to Maggie and Glen Ohmert for their editing expertise and friendship.

History of the Fur Trade and Fur Trapping

During the years of the mountain men and fur trappers, the history of the United States of America was exciting because enormous sweeps of land had opened up after the purchase of the Louisiana Territory.

Vast riches

The Louisiana Purchase was the very most important happening in President Thomas Jefferson's first administration. In 1803, he bought nearly 828,000 *square miles* of land from France for around $15 million.

Fifteen states would eventually come from this one tract of land. It extended the boundary of the United States from the Mississippi River to the Rocky Mountains and from the Gulf of Mexico to the Canadian border.

At this time, there were many American Indians living in this beautiful area and it had not been explored by white men in any organized fashion. In 1804, Lewis and Clark and their group made a great journey to see just what we had purchased.

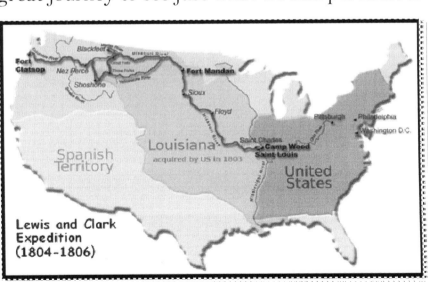

Lewis and Clark Expedition (1804-1806)

The land was rich in animals, lumber and ore, and good soil for farms and settlements - but that would all come about much later.

1954 postage stamp commemorating 150 year anniversary of the Lewis and Clark Expedition

Furs

Fur has been a great material for making clothing ever since man has been on the earth. It has two distinct layers. The outer layer sheds water and snow; the inner layer beneath keeps the animal warm. Animal pelts came to have great value for warmth *and for* style. Textures ranged from soft to coarse, and colors ranged from reds and browns to tans and grays.

Mountain Men and the Rendezvous

The fur trade had been underway with the French in Canada as early as the 1500's, so it was one of the earliest and most important industries as the riches of North America began to be developed. The people in Europe wanted furs, which only the rich could afford. Europeans found that mink, fox, and otter could be useful for style and warmth. Fashionable beaver fur hats in particular, which shed water, drove the fur trade.

French fishermen and explorers traded tools and trinkets and weapons to the Indians for furs. Then European men adopted a new fashion; they began wanting beaver furs for their felt hats.

Fur traders and fishermen traded with the Huron and Ottawa tribes, who got furs from other Indian groups. The French explorer Samuel de Champlain built a trading post where the city of Quebec is today.

Champlain arrives in Quebec

In the 1600's, the English had also begun getting furs from the Atlantic coastal areas. The Hudson's Bay Company, started by two English merchants were dealing with French fur traders who had the right to go for as many pelts (animal skins) as they could find.
Both the French and the English then began to want the fur trading

rights and began to fight over the area from the Mississippi River to the Alleghany Mountains. This led to a war between the French and the English. When the English won the war, the French left the colonies to the English.

Traders

Fur trading soon became big business after Lewis and Clark's expedition had explored and mapped the land of the Louisiana Purchase in 1804 and 1805. They had traveled all the way to the Pacific coast and had returned with their maps and reports of all there was to see.

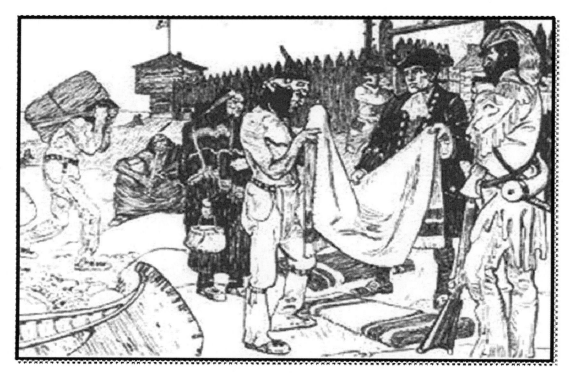

British trading blankets for furs

Big fur companies were formed and they advertised for white men to come and trap animals for their furs because the Indians did not really want to do this. Two of the companies were those run by John Jacob

Astor, the William H. Hudson Bay Company, and the Rocky Mountain Fur Company.

The mettle of the mountain man

Beaver pelts were obtained by trapping these animals in the rivers and streams. This was done in the colder months when the pelts were "prime". It was no easy task, especially when the fur trappers always had to keep an eye open for hostile enemies and sometimes even rivals from other fur companies!

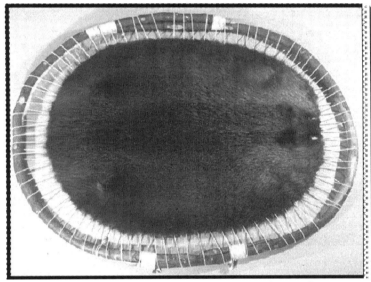

Beaver pelt stretched on a sapling frame

Concentration on the job at hand was a must. An accident in icy water or on a slippery bank could mean illness, even death. Weather was another element. Snow storms, blizzard-like conditions and low temperatures tested the mettle of the fur trappers. In the dead of winter, most everyone planned on heading to a fort or trading post by January.

The trappers knew of one another's exploits and challenges faced and survived. They also knew who had spent the winter out and didn't come in to a fort or post. At first, they might suspect the missing trapper had "gone under", but on seeing them in the spring or at the next rendezvous (large gathering of mountain men), the claps on the back and the greetings of "hullo, ol' hoss!" were a kind of celebration in itself.

Trappers headed for the rendezvous

Rendezvous – the connection
The rendezvous kept the mountain men in touch with one another and certainly provided an element of connection. They swapped stories of their adventures and of the native people they had encountered, "hostiles" and "friendlies", so men came to know the Indian tribes and their ways. There was a lot of storytelling going on at the rendezvous

Mountain Men and the Rendezvous

Jim Bridger came to be a great and well-known storyteller. Also, supplies were replenished; furs were traded or sold.

> The rendezvous described by Jim Beckwourth, a mountain man of the time:
> *"Mirth, songs, dancing, shouting, trading, running, jumping, singing, racing, target-shooting, yarns, frolic, with all sorts of extravagances that white men or Indians could invent."*

A week or two or three of rollicking rest was enjoyed as the ever-vigilant men could dance, drink strong drink, smoke their pipes, have contests for shooting, knife throwing, tomahawk throwing, running races, and anything else they could think of.

Brisk trading at the rendezvous

There was a "booshway" to see that the event had some organization with buyers and traders coming in, and supplies arriving, and the occasional fight that might break out. Generally, a strong sense of fairness, good humor, competition, and entertainment prevailed.

Before taking to the mountains again, plans were made and shared for the next rendezvous. Some of the locations for rendezvous were Pierre's Hole, Henry's Fork, Popo Agie, Bear Lake, Wind River, Cache Valley, Green River and Ham's Fork. Some locations were used over and over again as there was grass for the animals and game for the trappers. The area was most readily accessed through South Pass. The government was also interested in this area.

Men like Manual Lisa came here before the Lewis and Clark Expedition, or even before the Louisiana Purchase had been made. At the time, every group, i.e. British, French, and Americans, were all able to work here. There were no Mexicans.

Albert Bierstadt's impression of the Wind River area, the location of many rendezvous

Sometimes even the fun of the rendezvous was disturbed and disrupted by hostile Indians finding their enemies all in one place. Horses got stolen. Fighting might erupt. Sometimes there was a cold camp for the trappers for a while until things settled down with marauding Indians.

The last rendezvous was held in the Wind River area. Jim Bridger made his way there, coming in from the Yellowstone country. There were foreign guests and Joe Meek donned part of a suit of armor and entertained the Indians by galloping through the campground on horseback. There weren't nearly as many pelts, and in comparison to earlier rendezvous, it was a somber affair.

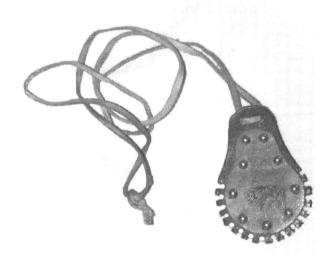

Cap pendant featuring a buffalo carving in the leather

Chapter 2

Land Claims and Fur Companies

The large body of water known as Hudson's Bay took its name originally from Henry Hudson, an early English explorer and sea captain. He made four voyages looking for a northern route between Europe and Asia. Although Hudson did not get to Asia, he did go farther north than any explorer had before him and several of the places he explored are named after him: Hudson Bay, Hudson Strait, and the Hudson River.

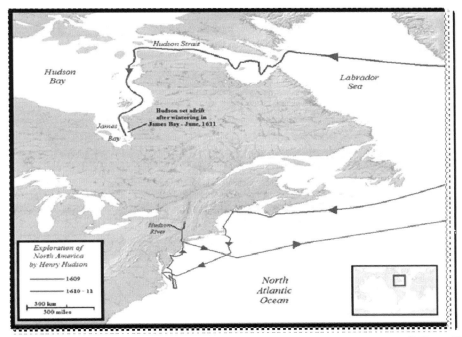

Henry Hudson's voyages of exploration; map courtesy of Jon Platek

On his fourth voyage, in 1610, Henry Hudson sailed his ship *Discovery* across the Atlantic and made landfall in North America off of Labrador. He then sailed through what is now known as Hudson Strait into Hudson Bay. The *Discovery* had a hard winter in James Bay on the south end of Hudson Bay. The miserable crew mutinied and put Hudson and his son into a boat with the crew members who remained loyal to him. Hudson and his group were never seen again. As a result of Henry

Hudson's last voyage, England claimed the region.

Sailing the "Discovery", Henry Hudson discovered and explored Hudson Bay

Hudson's Bay Company

Subsequent exploration led to the development of a fur trading firm in 1670, Hudson's Bay Company, one of the earliest and largest fur-trading posts in North America.

The vast area that forms the Hudson Bay watershed was known as Rupertsland, after Prince Rupert, cousin to King Charles of England. The company established trading posts and forts, placing them strategically at the mouths of many major rivers, with inland posts being developed as the company grew. The main "office" was at York Factory, a trading post way up in Canada on the great bay.

Hudson Bay drainage area (courtesy of Lokal_Profil)

Hudson's Bay Company's traders and trappers got an early start in the industry with the Native Americans of North America, both in Canada and the United States territories. They started trade with the indigenous people in the 1600's.

Indians at Hudson's Bay Company trading post

The network of forts and posts that Hudson's Bay Company had created gave the company some degree of authority when they faced competition later on.

Hudson's Bay was the largest private land owner and, when the fur trade waned, they adapted to new realities by selling provisions to prospectors and settlers.

Indeed, Hudson's Bay Company is the *oldest commercial operation in North*

America, having been in continuous operation for over 350 years. Today, the company has become an affiliation of numerous retail stores: Hudson's Bay, Home Outfitters, Lord and Taylor, Saks Fifth Avenue, Simpson Tower in Toronto, Canada.

Hudson's Bay Company flagship in downtown Toronto

Since 2008, the holding company NRDC, American Private Equity Firm, bought out several other short term ownerships. In a recent development, Hudson's Bay Company was dissolved as a company in 2012.

The Rocky Mountain Fur Company

General William Ashley started the Rocky Mountain Fur Company, giving many trappers their first chance at fur trapping. Sometimes called "Ashley's Hundred", the company was made up of free trappers. Ashley had placed an ad in a St. Louis newspaper in 1823 seeking "One hundred enterprising young men . . . to ascend the river Missouri to its source, there to be employed for one, two, or three years." Hugh Glass, William Sublette, Jim Bridger and Jedediah Smith, among many others, answered the ad. In this way, Ashley was the initiator of legends!

The North West Company

The North West Fur Company was formed in Montreal to compete with Hudson's Bay Company and to argue for their own rights. Eventually, The North West Fur Company merged with Hudson's Bay and this became a powerful group in its day. (While working with the Hudson's Bay Company, Peter Skene Ogden came as far south as Ogden, Utah, named after the trapper.)

North West Company - Coat of Arms

The American Fur Company

The American Fur Company was started by John Jacob Astor, a German immigrant. He was a challenge to the North West Fur Company and the Hudson's Bay Company, the two Canadian companies that had done the majority of fur trapping in the United States up until that time. By 1828, Astor's company had a monopoly on all the fur trading in the United States. He sold his company in 1834 and lived off his riches until his death 1847.

Self-employed trappers

The free trappers used a different arrangement. They worked not for someone else for wages, but for themselves, but they turned over a percent of their furs for transportation and for being outfitted by Ashley. His group also was among the first to employ white trappers instead of depending on the Indians for the furs.

Ashley held his first rendezvous on the eastern side of the Oregon country. He began the change from trading to trapping. He also began the event called the *rendezvous*. He most definitely was an entrepreneur. He sold out later to Jedediah Smith and went off to congress, which was his original goal.

Chapter 3

Forts in the Days of the Mountain Men

Fort Laramie before 1840

This chapter contains a partial list of the main forts in the west that were of key importance in the lives of the fur traders.

There were numerous forts built and used before the Louisiana Purchase that are not included in this chapter. Some forts existing at the time of the fur trappers were primarily built for protection from Indians and/or as military strongholds to insure protection. They are not mentioned significantly in most sources. Some forts mentioned in the list were begun by the early French or British traders and were used throughout the free trappers' times. They may have been included.

Forts significant to the mountain men are listed after the map below.

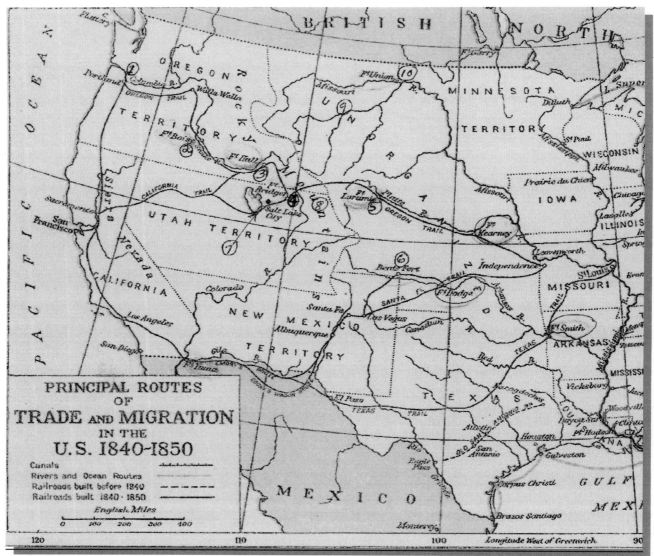

Map courtesy of heritage-history.com

The first nine forts listed below may be found on the map.

1. Fort Vancouver —Washington. Built in 1824-5 by Hudson's Bay Fur Company on the Columbia River *as a Fur trading outpost*. We are told that forts were built all along the course of this river.

2. Fort Boise – Southwestern Idaho. Built by Hudson's Bay Fur

Mountain Men and the Rendezvous

Company in 1834 *for the fur trade.*

3. Fort Hall – North of present-day Pocatello, Idaho on the Snake River in southern Idaho. Built by Nathaniel Jarvis Wyeth in the times of the *fur trappers-trading post and also for protection.*

4. Fort Bridger – Wyoming. There is much about this fort in the chapter on Jim Bridger.

5. Fort Laramie – Wyoming. Built by William Sublette and Robert Campbell, first called Fort William, but known by most by the name of the river nearby. *It was first an important fur trading post* and then later a military post. Several Indian treaties were signed here.

6. Bent's Fort – Colorado. Built by the Bent brothers, Charles and William, in 1833 in southeastern Colorado. It was an *important fur trading post* and later was protection for wagon trains. It *dominated the fur trade in Colorado for 15 years.* Unlike many other forts, Bent's Fort was constructed of adobe.

7. BuenaVentura – Utah. Built in 1845 by Miles Goodyear on the confluence of the Weber and Ogden Rivers. *Begun for the fur trappers, it ended up being a place of settlement.* This is now Ogden, Utah. It is the oldest settlement continuously occupied by Euro-Americans in Utah! Peter Skene Ogden, *fur trapper*, came there.

8. Fort Davey Crockett – Named for a hero of the Alamo. Built in 1837 on the Green River in Brown's Hole, near the present day Utah/Wyoming border, *active in the times of the mountain men and trappers.*

9. Fort Raymond - Montana Built by Manuel Lisa 1807 at the confluence of the Yellowstone and Big Horn rivers. Its purpose was for trading with the Crow Indians. This fort also went by the name Manuel's Fort.

Fort Union – Montana.. Fur trading fort built by Kenneth MacKenzie of the Upper Missouri Group of the American Fur Company. Situated on the north bank of the Missouri River 5 miles above the mouth of the Yellowstone River. Begun 1829, in operation 1833.

Fort Pierre - South Dakota. Built by Pierre Chouteau in 1832 as a trading post. *One of the jumping-off places for trappers going into the wilderness.*

Fort Uncompahgre – Colorado. Built by Antoine Robidoux on the Gunnison River, near present-day Montrose, in western Colorado. *Involved in the days of the fur trade.*

Fort Kit Carson – Utah. Near Ute Village at White Rocks, Utah. This was a Ute village. Built by Antoine Robidoux, 1832, *in the trading post era.*

Fort Uinta – Utah. Also near White Rocks, Utah. Built in 1837 by Antoine Robidoux *for the fur trade.*

Fort Phil Kearny – Wyoming. Built by Colonel Carrington and his troops in 1866 at the foot of the Bighorn Mountains. Known by the mountain men, but not as significant to them as were other forts of that time.

Fort Worth – Texas. Built by the Army in 1849 to protect border settlements. Known to the mountain men of that time, but not of importance to them.

Fort Bonneville – Wyoming. Built by L.E. Bonneville on the Green River near present-day Daniel, Wyoming. The trappers were derisive of it because it was so very cold there, but it was well-located from a military viewpoint.

Fort Kearny - Although this fort is present on the map, it was for emigrants on the Oregon Trail, and was not regularly used by the fur trappers.

Fort Smith - This fort is on the map, but it was used as a military post and became a settlement. This fort was not significant to the fur trappers.

Fort Osage – Kansas. 1808-1812, this fort served as a jumping-off place for western trappers and anyone going into the wilderness.

Fort McKenzie – Montana. Built in 1833 by David Dawson Mitchell as a *fur trade trading post*

Forts Vasquez, Jackson, and Lupton – Located along the Oregon Trail. *Built for trappers and mountain men*, these forts later served as protection for the wagon trains.

Fort Bridger in the 1840's

Liz Sartori

Food, Clothing and Shelter

A surprisingly long list of foods may be included here, keeping in mind that when mountain men were caught in snows, or lived among the Indians for a time, or got caught out and away from rendezvous for any reason, there were adjustments to their diets.

John C. Fremont's fourth expedition comes to mind. Stranded in terrible conditions, the men were eating soaked belts, or just they chewed on them, as is, *very* weak tea, sometimes without water for a time. If a mountain man was injured and alone, this affected what he might obtain – or not obtain. This is just one of several reasons for partnerships in the field.

The good stuff

But on a good day, or right after rendezvous with the supply wagon, or if the season was exceptionally good, well........Bacon, flour, molasses, sugar, dried apples, tea, and well, don't forget the tobacco and liquor.......and from the refrigerator in the wild: elk, deer (venison), buffler', bear, tongue, bighorn sheep, turkey, grouse, prairie chickens, ducks, geese, rabbits, berries, wild onions and other of the known herbs made their way into a stew. Fish, especially in the northwest was a mainstay and pemmican, an invention of the Indians, the mountain men learned about and made good use of.

To this list, the Indians would add dog, horse, grains, and almost anything else on the land as needed. They lived "waste not, want not." They used everything.

Clothing they could eat

Clothing was pretty basic. Trappers wore leather pants and jackets with fringes that had many uses - just cut one off a sleeve when needed, even eaten in times of starvation. Deer hide, tanned, generally.

Footwear most often was moccasins - a very durable leather slipper. Some of our footwear now closely mimics them. Sometimes a calico cloth shirt. Hats made from red fox, coon, mink or otter pelts, buffalo robes and blankets in winter and/or cold places up in the mountains. Bedding was of similar stuff, and soft furs. They often wintered in a fort or cabin,

Mountain Men and the Rendezvous

with simply more of the same – layers, as it were.

Much was obviously copied from the Indian, especially the moccasin. Different and the same, many a mountain man could tell you which Indians were around and about by their moccasin print evidence. They wore high leather moccasin boots in winter, sometimes fur-lined. Leggings were worn over all the rest. Blanket-coats, called *capotes*, protected them in winter.

The fancy stuff

Handcrafted necklace of cougar claws and antler beads

Adornment must be included here: bear claw and beaded necklaces, bracelets, bone pendants, talismans, feathers on the Indians and sometimes in the hair or hats of the mountain men.

A place to sleep

Shelter also included many variations. The mountain man, when he could, liked to be near a fort - not necessarily *in* the fort, however. He liked a cabin, if convenient or available. *In* the fort was for a harsh winter. Again, sometimes a copy of the Indian, a lean-to, with boughs for a bed and, in summer, no cover was okay.

Indian teepees, painting Karl Bodmer

Travois

Some wintered with the Indians in their brush houses or the buffalo hide tepee. The Plains Indians always took their tepees along on a travois to haul them to their next location following the buffalo.

Brush lean-to

Sometimes the key was location, for example up against a rock cliff, or a place with an "escape route".

The best one I know of is Liver-Eating Johnson's cabin with a hidden cave that ran into the next canyon - the location where he poisoned the attackers with biscuits laced with strychnine while Johnson and his friends made their escape. Twenty-nine enemies felled in one night!

Mountain man re-enactor; courtesy of Robert Lawton

The real thing, Seth Kinman, 1864

How to Trap a Beaver In the Rocky Mountains

In the vast regions of the American West were many rivers and streams. Many beaver lodges were built in those streams and many beavers occupied those homes.

Then came an unexpected, and unwelcome, visitor – the mountain man.

The mountain man readied his horse and his pack mules, his supplies, rifle and hunting knife and half a dozen or so traps, double spring steel with chains, and then rode into the wilderness.

*Beaver lodge - warm and dry inside;
surrounded by water for safety*

He set his traps under water. They are attached to a wooden stake hammered into the bottom of the stream and they are baited with castoreum, a smelly musk taken from the glands of a beaver. The beaver is caught in the trap and drowned.

#3 beaver trap

The next morning, the trapper visits his traps, hauls the beaver out of the water and skins it.
He stretches the hide on a hoop-like form to dry. When it is dry, he folds it with the fur-side inside. It then becomes part of a bundle of about 20 skins, which he transports on his pack mules.

Trappers setting their traps in shallow water

What happens next depends on the time of year, the plans, and the weather conditions. The bundles may be cached (hidden) until taken to rendezvous, taken to a river boat, or carried overland for some time.

When the pelts go to the rendezvous, traders, agents of the fur companies and trappers bargain for supplies, ball and powder, trinkets, liquor, needles and thread and many other useful or fanciful items.

Crusty and tough – a mountain man on his way to trade his pelts

Trappers headed out to the beaver streams

Chapter 6

Peter Skene Ogden ~ Trader, Explorer, Company Man

More is known about Peter Skene Ogden's (1790-1854) parentage than about those of many of the other fur trappers. His father was Chief Justice Isaac Ogden of Quebec, but all we know about his mother is her name, Sarah Hanson. Peter was descended from a 1600's emigrant from Great Britain.

His ancestors came to the American colony of New Jersey and to Long Island. His father and grandfather were loyalists during the American Revolution who, after they had taken a trip to Britain, returned to North America, this time settling in Quebec, which by that time was governed by the British. Peter's brother Charles was a lawyer and politician in eastern Canada.

Place names

Many places bear the name of Peter Ogden, including Ogden, Utah, Ogden River, in Utah; Ogden State Scenic Viewpoint in Jefferson County, Oregon; Ogden Point, Victoria, British Columbia, and several schools in Washington, Oregon, and British Columbia. Interestingly, a restaurant in Las Vegas at the Downtown Grand sports the name Stewart & Ogden.

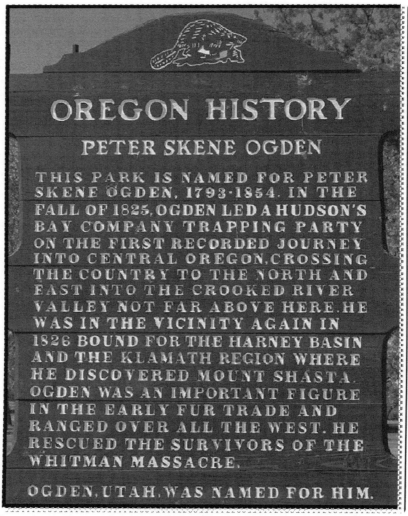

Marker at Peter Skene Ogden State Park, near Bend, Oregon

International Career

Ogden was a fur trader in British Columbia and in the American West. He explored parts of what are now Oregon, Washington, Nevada, California, Utah, Idaho and Wyoming.

Peter Ogden started off his career with the American Fur Company, and then joined the North West Company in 1809, only six years after the Louisiana Purchase from France. Lewis and Clark finished their western explorations in '04 and '05. Ogden's first post was at Il-a-la-Crosse, Saskatchewan and then a post 100 miles south of there at Green Lake, Saskatchewan. He married Julia Rivet/Reava, a Nez Perce woman.

Strife

Ogden was in competition with Hudson's Bay Company and got into physical altercations with some of its traders. It is said he killed an

Trading at Hudson's Bay Company, Canada

Indian who traded with the Hudson's Bay Company. While this action was not unacceptable to many, the Hudson's Bay people put up such a tizzy that Ogden was moved further west to avoid further altercations. The strife between the two companies ended when they joined together in 1821. Ogden was then appointed chief trader for the Snake River Country of Hudson's Columbia department in 1823.

The Great Salt Lake, painting by Thomas Moran

Explorations

With this, more than six years of explorations began. Ogden led a group east to Montana's Bitterroot River and south to the Bear River in Utah. He then traveled south from the Columbia River to the Deschutes River in Oregon, then on through the Blue Mountains to the Snake River. Then in 1826-27, Ogden undertook a vast journey from Walla Walla, Washington to the Deschutes River, Klamath Lake, and nearly all the way to Mount Shasta in northern California.

The next two years, 1828 and 1829, found Ogden's party exploring the Great Salt Lake and the Weber River Drainage, where Ogden, Utah and the Ogden River still bear his name. He explored the Great Basin, following the Humboldt River to present-day Nevada. The party then went along the eastern Sierra Nevada, the Mojave Desert of Mexican California, even reaching the north shore of the Gulf of California in Baja California. These explorations were a successful undertaking for the Hudson's Bay Company. Ogden truly traveled north to south and north again, probably crossing more parallels than any other trader or trapper.

Ogden established a post in British Columbia, Fort Simpson, and managed a post on the south coast of Alaska. Throughout the 1840's, he administered the fur trade at Fort Vancouver.

Fort Vancouver about 1845

Ogden competed successfully against the American Fur Company by working with local tribes, i.e. the Cayuse. These relationships paid off in many ways. Knowing their ways, Ogden was able to successfully negotiate with the Cayuse for the lives of 49 settlers who had been taken as slaves following the Whitman massacre.

Peter Skene Ogden ended up in Oregon City with one of his Native American wives. He died there, after writing *Traits of American Indian Life and Character by a Fur Trader,* a book that is still read today for its authentic historical value.

Clearly, Ogden's life of adventure took him in a very different direction from the lives of his patrician forbearers in Quebec.

Etienne Provost – Trader and Trapper

Etienne Provost (pronounced Pro-vo), born in 1785, was one of the earliest fur traders. Because he lived a long life for his times, 65 years, his active life spanned almost the entire fur trade era. Provost died only 10 years after the waning of the fur trade.

Provost's life was distinguished by numerous noteworthy accomplishments. He escorted John James Audubon's natural history expedition of 1843. Provost is immortalized on the *This Is the Place Monument*, just outside Salt Lake City, Utah. The Provo River, Provo Canyon, and Provo, Utah, all in central Utah, are named after this adventuresome man.

Early adventures

A French Canadian fur trader, Provost worked in the American southwest before Mexico gained its independence. His company was headquartered in Taos, New Mexico, and he was very active with the Indians in the Green River drainage and in the central part of Utah.

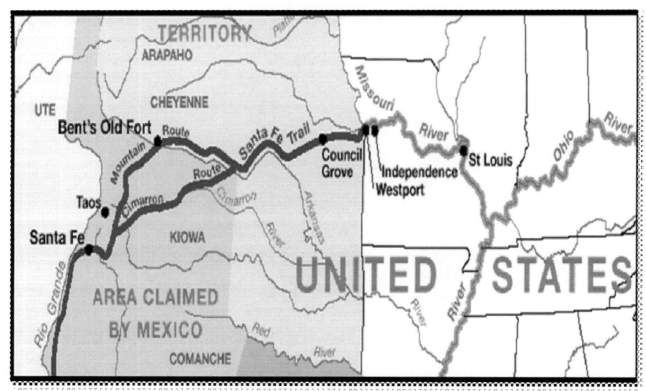

Etienne Provost's Company was headquartered in Taos, New Mexico

Some argue that Provost was the first man of European descent to see the Great Salt Lake – instead of Jim Bridger. He was on its shores in 1824-25. Given the dates of these two men, this is certainly possible. *Qui sait?* Who knows? Certainly Provost and Antoine Robidoux became the most famous of the Taos trappers in Utah.

The French Connection

It is a fact that Provost was born in Quebec, but little is known about his early life there. Perhaps he was not of notable parentage or his family didn't keep written records. We do know that he lived in St. Louis for ten years, partnering with Joseph Philibert. He left there with Auguste

Chouteau and Jules DeMun, all men with French names.

Let us note the influence of the French that is still evident today in place names. The French explorer Jacques Cartier claimed Canada for France in the 16th century. Two centuries later, New France occupied an area stretching from Hudson's Bay to the mouth of the Mississippi and from Acadia to the Rocky Mountains.

As a result, the western states of the United States have a plethora of French place names describing the land or honoring the founder. For instance, Oregon was "Ouragon", meaning "hurricane".

The suffix "ville", meaning "town", is common throughout the United States.

A few examples of French names in Idaho are:

- Bonneville, named after the French trapper and explorer
- Coeur d'Alene, "heart of the awl"
- Grangeville, "barn city"
- Pierre's Hole, "Peter's Valley".

Several Native American tribes were given French names, notably *Nez Perce*, meaning "pierced nose." And we can't forget the French word for the Indian "travois" that carried the Plains Indians' gear from place to place as they followed the buffalo.

Having explored the wide-ranging linguistic marks of the French explorers, trappers and traders, we return to Provost's adventures.

Misunderstandings

In Santa Fe, New Mexico, Provost was twice put in jail. Clearly, the Mexicans misread the mountain men's intentions, thinking they had political ambitions and designs on claiming land for the government.

The mountain men were unconcerned about any country's borders or politics, but the Mexicans were understandably suspicious.

Attack

About 1822, Provost returned to New Mexico, partnering with Francois Leclerc to trap the Uintah Basin. His party was attacked by Snake Indians in October, 1824 at the Jordan River near the Great Salt Lake.

Santa Fe, New Mexico in the early days

At that time, the Jordan River was known as Proveau's Fork.

Provost had met with Shoshoni Chief Bad Gocha. When the trappers laid down their guns to smoke the peace pipe, Bad Gocha's men attacked them suddenly, catching them completely off guard. Eight men were killed, but Provost was not among them. We are told by some sources that this attack was motivated by the killing of a Shoshoni chief by a member of Ogden's Hudson's Bay Company. Bad blood multiplies misfortunes.

Forts on the lakes

Provost built forts on Utah Lake and Great Salt Lake. A replica of Provost's fort now stands on the western end of Provo, nearly out to the shores of Utah Lake.

Provost's trappers had come before the Rocky Mountain Fur Company trappers. It is interesting that Provost met Peter Skene Ogden of Hudson's Bay Company in Weber Canyon.

Fort Utah on the Timpanogas - Valley of the Great Salt Lake

Ogden had come south with his party from the Hudson's Bay Company's Flathead Post near Eddy, Montana. Ashley had boated down the Green River and traveled up the Duchesne and Strawberry Rivers to present–

day Fruitland, where he met Provost.

In those days before Ashley began the "collect and resupply in the field method", furs were brought all the way to St. Louis. Provost returned to St. Louis in 1826 and became a trapper in the American Fur Company of John Jacob Astor. He did his own trapping, as well as leading American Fur Company trappers on trips up the Missouri River.

Guide

Provost led men on ventures of the upper Missouri River, while at the same time managing to carry on his own trapping adventures.

Shoshone teepees, mid-19th century

Three years later, Provost married, but continued bringing American Fur Company parties to the yearly rendezvous until 1838. He kept up his recruiting and continued guiding a variety of expeditions.

For many years, until his death in 1850, Provost lived in St. Louis, Missouri.

Ceran St. Vrain - Fur Trapper, Trader, Businessman, Politician, Military Aide

Ceran St. Vrain knew the fur trappers of the southwest - Provost, Bent, Antoine Robidoux, Wooten, and others. He worked "in the trenches", so to speak, with traders and Indians and rose to prominence in the New Mexico Territory.

What we know

Ceran St. Vrain, born in 1802, lived a long, full life for his time, living until 1870. More would now be known about him had more of his paper trail survived. Still, we do know that his father, Jacques St. Vrain, was born in Flanders and migrated to St. Louis a few years after his own father had fled the French Revolution.

When he was in his teens, Ceran St. Vrain's father died and the boy went to live with the Pratte family. There he became acquainted with the fur trade, Pratte being involved in two trading companies. As a result, Ceran got into Santa Fe trading when he was in his 20's. Things did not go well at first. After he made it to Taos, he hadn't sold much and expected to sell the remainder to Provost and Le Clerc. He also had business dealings with Guerin and Baillio. He spent the winter in Taos and learned to speak Spanish so well he did not need an interpreter in business dealings. He also knew "Peg-Leg Smith", who was not yet "Peg-Leg", just Tom.

In the Gila River expedition, St. Vrain was the leader of one of the four groups engaged in private trade. They also expected to trap the Colorado and Gila Rivers for beaver.

Fashionable fur hats drove the fur trade

Calamities

The next expedition was headed up by Pratte and Milton Sublette and Tom Smith were also in the group. They collected 300 beaver skins. Unfortunately, Pratte was bitten by a dog and died of hydrophobia. After this, everyone looked to St. Vrain, as he had good leadership qualities. He made himself accountable to pay the workers overtime wages. It was St. Vrain who looked after Tom Smith when an Indian arrow took out Tom's leg, seeing after his comfort and needs.

They wintered on the Green River near the Utes. A wonderful spring trapping season yielded a thousand beaver so a few of the party set off for St. Louis. However, because they were low on ammunition, they turned back when Indian evidence looked intimidating.

Profits

Selling in St. Louis was too slow to suit him, so he sold wholesale and received $10,000 for goods he'd paid $3,000 for. He turned the money over to Pratte & Company. On his return, Ceran St. Vrain made a deal with Charles Bent.

Those two did well together. While Ceran stayed in New Mexico selling, Bent went to St. Louis to purchase more goods. While he was in New Mexico, St. Vrain arranged for dual citizenship, becoming a naturalized American citizen and he maintained a home in Taos.

The two formed a new fur company and built a fort, Fort William, to trade with the Cheyennes and Arapahos. A year later, they built Bent's Fort for trade with still more Indian tribes. There was a Fort St. Vrain, too, on the South Platte. They welcomed many at the forts, including Colonel Henry Dodge with his 120 military men.

Dollars and Sense

St. Vrain sent a group to trade with the Indians in the Sioux lands and returned with $25,000 in pelts. Later, they purchased $13,000 worth of

Bent's Fort in its heyday

goods and supplies from the American Fur Company. While Ceran was shipping his furs down the Arkansas River, he met up with Charles Bent and his fourteen wagons. Captain Phillip St. George Cooke and his troops were escorting the caravan. (Cooke was a Union General in the American Civil War, sometimes called "Father of the U.S. Cavalry".) During the Mexican-American War, Cooke led the Mormon Battalion from Santa Fe to California.)
He spent the winter at Bent's Fort, and much later in the year, St. Vrain and Bent welcomed Colonel Kearny to the fort.

William Bent

Both Bent and St. Vrain became interested in developing land grants. They obtained a four million acre tract. Then, when the Mexican War became imminent, the two men quickly left for St. Louis. Bent returned first and was appointed first civil governor of New Mexico. U.S. occupation of the territory led to Mexican and Pueblo Indians' revolt and the subsequent death of Charles Bent.

Work, work, work

St. Vrain began to diversify his businesses. He built sawmills, supplying lumber to Santa Fe's commissioners of public buildings, built a flour mill in Mora, later supplied the military with grain, beef and flour. Later St. Vrain became the designated printer in the territory, and, still later, he was named lieutenant colonel of mounted volunteers.

Several months after the Civil War had begun, St. Vrain became colonel of the First New Mexican Calvary. He then moved up to fill the position of one of the three representatives to the Territorial Convention. But, in the run for lieutenant governor, he lost to Manuel Alvarez.

From 1855 until his death at age sixty-eight, Mora, New Mexico, was his home. He was buried by the Masons.

Bill Williams – Trapper, Scout, Guide, Interpreter, Indian Fighter

Old Bill Williams got his nickname when he was only 37. It had to be an endearment! He was respected by all the mountain men for his savvy in the field and for his knowledge of Indians. He led masterfully and was helpful to anyone wanting to know more about the west. He knew French, Spanish, and many Indian dialects.

Adventuresome youth

William Williams, born in 1787 in North Carolina, was the fourth of nine children. Both parents were of Welsh ancestry and had come from Virginia. Joseph, his father, fought for the side of the colonies during the Revolutionary War until he received a bad wound in his leg. Their capable mother, Sarah Musick, taught the children - the Baptist doctrine and even Latin.

The family answered an invitation to the Upper Louisiana Territory from the governor of the Spanish posts. They decided to move west. With much arduous travel, they arrived at Whiteside Station, Northwest Territory, near St. Louis. The Spanish government gave Joseph 680 acres of land across the Missouri.

The boys ranged far and wide and at one point found themselves at a village of Osage Indians. At age 16, Will, as his family called him, decided to stay there and learn their ways. He learned the language and hunted with them, married one of their own, and had two daughters, Sarah and Mary.

Good with languages

He was 25 years old when the war of 1812 began and he volunteered with Captain Callaway's Company C of the Mounted Rangers. He was back in the Osage village in December of 1813 when his second daughter, Mary, was born.

Bill interpreted for George Sibley, Indian agent, at Fort Osage. Bill was official interpreter for a sub-station under Paul Baillio. When New England missionaries arrived in the Osage country with the government's blessing, he felt impatient with civilization and with Christianity as he saw it acted out there. He left as the whites began to crowd in. He did help the missionaries with his 2000-word dictionary, which displayed his intellectual ability.

Guide

Bill became a guide to Generals Henry Atkinson and Edmund Gaines and to other army officers touring in a military inspection. It was off-putting to the missionaries because they knew he wasn't interpreting correctly what they were trying to say to the Indians. His two additional wives also troubled the missionaries. The Osage approved, as it was their custom. The missionaries prayed for him.

Independent trader

Bill became an independent trader with the Indians and prospered. After defending three Osage warriors, he headed for the Rocky Mountains. He worked with William Ashley's party under Jed Smith, but there was Indian hostility.

Bill escaped from some Blackfeet after killing four and then floating downriver to camp on a raft. He joined a government expedition under George Sibley, helping to make a trade road from Fort Osage to Santa Fe. He was an interpreter, a runner, and a hunter. The party was guided through the Sangre de Cristo Mountains by Francisco Largo, a civilized Comanche, and arrived in Taos late in 1825. Old Bill did well trapping the Rio Grande. When he returned to Taos, he began gambling and ended his time there working with the road commission.

Trapper

With his old buddies, Williams trapped and skirmished with the Blackfeet. Suffering serious wounds, they made camp on the Yellowstone at the Bighorn.

When he was working alone, Apaches captured Old Bill and turned him loose in the desert - naked, afoot, with no weapons. After he had travelled 160 miles, Zunis found him and took care of him, treating him like royalty.

After making it back to Taos, he left with the party of Pratte, St. Vrain, and several other men. This was the trip on which Pratte was bitten by a rabid dog, sickened, and died of hydrophobia. They wintered near the Green River, then, when the group split up in April, he went back to Taos.

An early Zuni governor

Explorer

More travels, more trapping, he then lived with Antonia Baca, a widow with three children and in about 1834 a son, José, was born to them. Later, Bill organized an expedition to California to explore Mexican land, leisurely hunting and visiting people along the way. In our day, Bill Williams would have been an anthropologist!

In their travels, the group came upon the Grand Canyon, beheld a large petrified forest, and wintered in a Walapai village. Off again into unfamiliar land, they made it to the Great Salt Lake, and after many more miles, to Lake Coeur d'Alene, where Old Bill outfitted for the trapping season.

He and a partner ran a fifty-trap line, yielding 600 beaver skins. Thence on to the summer rendezvous on the Green River, where he sold his furs, then to Bent's Fort to lead the Bent-St. Vrain wagon train to Santa Fe.

Bent's old fort

Now, at over 50, he was traveling all over, but the trapping trade was waning by 1838. His trapping was sporadic and he lived among the Utes to learn of them, also enjoying several intimate relationships.

He decided to visit the folks back in Missouri, but changed his mind and instead went a year later, seeing his daughter Mary and her daughter Susan, then his aging mother and his brothers and sisters. He must have had some tales to tell!

Life among the Indians

In 1842, Bill outfitted again out of St. Louis, with a partner, recruiting six others. They traded at a Cheyenne village, then Sioux villages east of Laramie. Encountering a band of Blackfeet looking for trouble, they killed all of them. They met Bill's old friend Washakie and his Shoshones and, because of the recent deaths of two trappers and the theft of Shoshone horses, they warred with the Blackfeet aggressors. In the fights and greater battles, the enemy lost 21 men, many horses, and some property; the allies lost only *one* Shoshoni. This they celebrated, or at least recalled, for a century.

Old Bill then organized another trapping trip of two years' duration. Before the group disbanded in 1845, they were attacked by Modoc Indians and the trappers lost three men; the Modocs lost thirty - a disproportionate loss for the Modocs.

Misadventures and a tragedy

Williams joined up with one of the Fremont expeditions and they traveled far until, after they'd gotten to the Great Salt Lake, a disagreement between the guides and Fremont about the crossing of the Salt Desert caused Bill to leave the party. This was Fremont's third trip.

Bill was called to serve with other mountain men scouting and guiding for Major W.W. Reynolds in a military campaign. Utes and Apaches had been troubling the northern New Mexico settlements. In a fierce battle, the Indians were soundly routed; thirty-six Indians were killed and two soldiers, no doubt due to a difference in the weapons on the opposing sides. Many on both sides were wounded. It is said that Bill fought gallantly and took a shot in the arm.

A terrible decision

John C. Fremont found Bill again on the Arkansas River and wanted him to guide his group for his fourth expedition. They left the next day. Fremont wanted to follow an unknown route between two other routes. Fitzpatrick thought it impossible; Bill knew the extreme difficulty this would pose, especially during the winter, so he tried to lead them through a less formidable crossing, but Fremont rejected his proposal and continued to argue with Williams.

One inexperienced guide told Fremont that he'd found a wagon road. Wanting to believe this, Fremont chose to listen to this voice of less experience.

This dangerous decision developed into tragedy. The group became isolated for five days. Men were snow-blind and suffering frostbite. Food was gone and a mule died. They fell back to a previous camp and sent four men for help.

Political poster extolling the triumphs of John C. Fremont

Bill and three others subsisted on a hawk, an otter, parched boots, belts and knife scabbards. One man died.

Very fortunately, one of the men was able to kill a deer. As they revived, Fremont and three others arrived on Ute horses, having left men frozen and starving to death in the mountains. Ten men and 120 mules were dead. Twenty-three men were crippled from their severe hardships. Some of them would never recover, and suffered the rest of their lives from their tragic misadventure.

Old Bill, with the expedition's doctor, went back to recover the doctor's medical equipment and supplies. They managed to get the equipment, but were shot and killed, probably by Utes.

An 8 foot sculpture of Bill Williams in Williams, Arizona

Chapter 10

Joseph Walker – Pushing America's Manifest Destiny

Joseph Walker was an experienced frontiersman who found a way to California from the rendezvous country that others would follow. He knew the Great Basin better than any other man.

For fifty years, Walker was a part of America's manifest destiny. He loved to explore new territory and make new trails. He was a lieutenant to Benjamin Bonneville and led his group on a journey of exploration to

California. For many years, he broke trails to the west and southwest. Importantly, he was the one to discover a gap in the Sierra Nevada Mountains which was eventually named after him.

Joseph Walker and his party were the first non-indigenous people to see Yosemite and the redwoods (sequoias) of California. How thunderstruck he must have been at the majestic trees that had been growing for centuries, even millennia, before he happened on the awesome sight. A member of the group, Zenas Leonard, wrote in his journal that streams from the valley rim dropped "from one lofty precipice to another, until they are exhausted in rain below. Some of these precipices appeared to us to be more than a mile high." Much to the dismay of the explorer and to history buffs ever since, journals relating to the Walker party were destroyed in a print shop fire in Philadelphia in 1839.

Beginnings

Walker began life in Tennessee. At age 21, he moved to Missouri, living on the then-frontier of the United States. The call of the fur trade, trapping, and hunting brought him into an expedition to New Mexico and the Rocky Mountains. As luck would have it, he happened upon his brother Joel along the way. Joel was astounded at his brother's Indian-like looks.

Joseph guided groups and found lost folks, getting them where they needed to be. He spent time on the Santa Fe Trail and signed Indian treaties in the Southwest.

Walker was the first sheriff of Jackson County, Missouri. He had the honor of naming Independence, which became the county seat. The 6-foot-tall Joseph could look intimidating, which probably helped him plenty in this chosen profession.

He left law enforcement to guide a pack train into Cherokee country, meeting Benjamin Bonneville at Fort Gibson. He signed on for Bonneville's exploring trip into the Rocky Mountains. The party left from Fort Osage, travelling here and there: the Platte River, the Sweetwater, the Green River, the Salmon River, Montana, and a finally rendezvous on the Green River. They wandered west toward California and were to make a wonderful discovery in the Sierra Nevadas.

A mild winter

In their wanderings, they discovered Yosemite in winter snow, and the California redwoods. Wintering in California, they revelled in its mild climate.

Yosemite Valley

Bonneville's party, trading in Monterey, found horses. With some help from two friendly Indians, they discovered a pass, later named Walker Pass. It is the northern-most snow-free pass across the Sierra Nevada Mountains.

After all that, they still managed to make it to summer rendezvous. Washington Irving's book about Benjamin Bonneville contains maps and information provided by Joseph Walker.

Guide to the Pacific Ocean

Walker guided a group that wanted to start a settlement on the Pacific coast, led by Joseph Chiles. At one point, the group divided and Joseph led his half through Walker Pass. He came back over the "Old Spanish Trail", once established by the Spanish fathers. There he met John C. Fremont and agreed to guide him to Bent's Fort.

Walker guided groups on the Oregon Trail; he also found the time to take Fremont on his third expedition. When the group split up, Joseph took his group south. The two groups met up again in the San Joaquin Valley.

When Fremont made some unwise and dangerous choices, Joseph asked for and got his discharge. He then went after horses for the U. S. Army that were sorely needed for the Spanish American War.

When Walker and Bonneville split up, Walker spent some time with the American Fur Company. Alfred Jacob Miller, a well-known artist made two paintings of Joseph. He titled one "Bourgeois Walker and His Squaw". Bourgeois, you may remember, means "boss".

Bourgeois and Squaw, painting by Alfred Jacob Miller, 1837

A man of integrity, Walker traded for horses while others stole them. He was angry when someone killed two Indians which caused later troubles. On a trip to California he sold over 400 pounds of beaver with his partner, Henry Fraeb, another mountain man, and they made over $1,100. When Fraeb was killed by Indians, Joseph teamed up with two more mountain men, Jim Bridger and Louis Vasquez, and went trapping and trading out of Fort Bridger.

Matthew Field, a newspaperman of the time, after meeting Joseph Walker, described him as a "fine old mountain man – healthy, grey-haired, and eagle-eyed".

A man for all seasons

Walker travelled back and forth, hither and yon, taking one job after another when each was completed. He sold horses to the army, carried letters from emigrants to St. Louis, headed west again and met up with Sublette and Tom Fitzpatrick, took a band of horses from California to Utah, then returned and sold meat to the miners during the gold rush. He went to ranching for a while. Next up was gold mining near Prescott, Arizona. In that region, a number of things are named after him, such as Walker River, Walker Lake, and others.

Joseph Walker spent the rest of his years on a ranch in California.

Joseph Walker at about 60 years of age

Liz Sartori

Chapter 11

Hugh Glass - Frontiersman, Frontier Folk Hero

Believed to be Hugh Glass

Hugh Glass was a member of Ashley's American Fur Company's free trappers. He is famous in frontier folklore because he got mauled by a grizzly bear, got left for dead by his friends, and made it back to Fort Kiowa with wounds, and without weapons for almost the entire grueling journey. A desire for revenge – and a lot of luck - may have been what kept him alive in such adverse conditions. In the end, Glass did lose his life to Indians in 1833.

We don't know the exact date Glass was born, though historians are saying around 1780 – so he lived a very full 53 years of life. There is a monument to Hugh Glass near where he fought the grizzly, at Shadehill Reservoir on the forks of the Grand River.

Hugh Glass explored the Upper Missouri River in present-day North Dakota, South Dakota, and Montana.

In 1822, like so many others, Glass responded to Ashley's ad in the newspaper. Among the other men who responded to this famous ad were Jim Beckwourth, Thomas Fitzpatrick, David Jackson, John Fitzgerald, William Sublette, Jim Bridger, and Jedediah Smith - the stuff of legends, every one.

In the trek with Ashley's Hundred, Glass was a hard-working fur trapper. He was wounded in a battle with Arikaras, or "Rees", as the mountain men called the tribe. Later, he traveled with 13 men to relieve the traders at Fort Henry at the mouth of the Yellowstone River.

Near the forks of the Grand River, in August of 1823, Glass was scouting for game and was out ahead of the group when a mama griz with two cubs to protect charged him before he could fire his rifle. While Glass fought back with a knife, that nervous mama raked him repeatedly with her claws. She then violently threw the unfortunate trapper to the ground.

Glass got help from the ever-faithful and fearless Jim Bridger and John Fitzgerald, who had finally caught up with him, but he was terribly mauled and lying unconscious.

Andrew Henry was there also and thought Glass would have no chance of surviving. He left two volunteers - 19-year-old Bridger, and 23-year-old Fitzgerald – to stay with Glass until his end and then bury him. No one thought it would be long.

Drawing by Charles M. Russell depicting grizzly attack on Hugh Glass

The volunteers said later that they had been interrupted by Arikara Indians while at their grim task of digging poor Glass' grave. They lit out with Glass' rifle, knife, and equipment and reported him dead.

Glass came to and found himself alone with a broken leg, bear-injured ribs, and numerous wounds beginning to fester. He began to *crawl* toward Fort Kiowa, 200 miles away. It took him 6 weeks overland, avoiding dangerous water-ways to reach the Cheyenne River. To avoid gangrene, he even let maggots eat out his decaying wounded flesh.

He ate wild berries and roots, and leftovers from a buffalo calf that had been downed by wolves.

Glass floated downriver on a raft he had struggled to put together.

With food and some weapons given to him by friendlies, Glass finally reached Fort Kiowa and safety – and a lengthy recuperation. 'Tis true: "Whatever doesn't kill you, makes you stronger." He lived to fight another day – against some Arikaras.

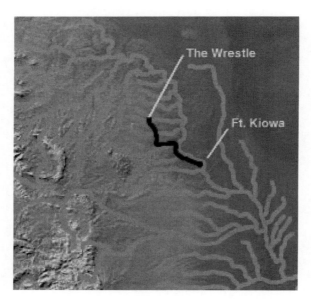

Glass struggled 100 miles overland then rafted down to Fort Kiowa

When he had arrived at the fort with vengeance in his heart, Glass had spared Bridger because of his young age. Fitzgerald he spared because he'd joined the army, knowing that killing a U.S. Soldier meant the death sentence.

Later, Glass and a party of trappers were looking for a new trapping route for Ashley. Glass' party started off in a bull boat and landed among what they at first thought were friendlies, but they soon had to run for it – er – float for it - in their bull boat. Marx and Dutton escaped but More and Chapman were killed. Glass hid behind a rock and then joined some Sioux who were on their way back to the fort.

He again returned to the frontier as a trapper and trader. Then he became a hunter for the garrison at Fort Union. Hugh Glass was killed on the Yellowstone River in the winter of 1833 in an attack by the Arikara.

Liz Sartori

Jedediah Smith – Trail Blazer

Jedediah Smith was Ashley's right-hand man and is noted as an explorer *and* a fur trapper. Smith distinguished himself with many firsts: He was the first to take a route to California that others thought was impossible. He was the first to recognize the best, most natural way to go to the Oregon country. He was the first to travel overland to California, blazing the trail from Great Salt Lake to California, and he was the first to cross the Sierra Nevada Mountains.

Smith was noted as a religious Bible-reading man among folks who weren't in the habit of doing any of that. He always carried his Bible with him and was considered the one to call on for the prayer at burials.

Early life

Jedediah was born in New York, but his family moved to Erie County, Pennsylvania when he was a child of eight. At age 18, he moved again, this time to Ohio with his "pioneering" family. Five years later, he went to St. Louis just in time to answer William Ashley's ad to go up the Missouri to the mouth of the Yellowstone.

Said Jedediah,

> *"I wanted to be the first to view a country on which the eyes of a white man had never gazed and to follow the course of rivers that run through a new land."*

Brave Fighter

Jedediah Smith travelled with Andrew Henry and spent that first winter near the mouth of the Mussellshell River. In the spring, Henry sent Jedediah back to Ashley to tell him of their need for horses. On the way back, a group of Arickaree Indians (the mountain men called them "Rees") attacked the party and it was soon discovered how brave and courageous a fighter Jedediah Smith proved to be. He volunteered to go get help from Henry. Smith joined with Colonel Leavenworth of the U.S. Army and with Ashley's men and members of the Missouri Fur Company to take care of the Indians.

Smith searched for new beaver country with William Sublette and Thomas Fitzpatrick south of the Yellowstone. Leaving from Fort Kiowa, they traveled westward into Sioux Indian lands. West of the Black Hills, Smith was mauled by a grizzly bear. (The mountain men called them a "grizz".) His head and face got horribly messed up and an ear was pretty much torn off. Again, courage was called for as Jim Clyman sewed up the gashes and, at Smith's instructions, sewed his ear back on. After that, Jedediah wore his hair even longer to cover up his many scars.

During Smith's second winter, the group lived among the Crow Indians (called "friendlies" by the mountain men) and the Crows told them about a river teeming with beaver. So, in early spring, they moved out and down to the Sweetwater, over the Continental Divide through South Pass and by March they had reached the Green River with its water flowing westward.

Breaking into two groups, Smith took half of the men downriver with him while Tom Fitzpatrick took the other half upriver. All of them harvested abundant beaver pelts.

> I started into the mountains, with the determination of becoming a first-rate hunter, of making myself thoroughly acquainted with the character and habits of the Indians, of tracing out the sources of the Columbia River and following it to its mouth, and of making the whole profitable to me, and I have perfectly succeeded. —Jedediah Smith

Ashley followed them because he had gotten word that the Hudson's Bay Fur Company men were in the same area. Iroquois Indians were being threatened by the Shoshones so they made a deal with Jedediah Smith to get them to the Flathead Post on the Columbia. For successfully accomplishing this, they gave Smith 105 pelts.

Money Talks

Peter Skene Ogden, with the Hudson's Bay Company, was in charge of the Flathead Post and when they met up, Smith and six other men went with his group to trap on the Snake River. They also came upon some of Ashley's men who had wintered in Cache Valley. A party from Taos led by Etienne Provost met up with them, too, making quite a group.

Some of the British trappers joined the American trappers, too, because they noticed that they could get better fur prices that way.

Everyone spread out in all directions, planning to meet for rendezvous at the beginning of July at Henry's Fork above the Uinta Mountains. Nearly 9,000 pounds of beaver were brought in by Ashley and Smith. After that rendezvous, Smith had a part interest in the company.

Smith wintered among the Pawnees and then met up with Ashley on the Platte at Grand Island along the Oregon Trail. Later, they met in Cache Valley for the summer of 1826 and had trapped even more beaver than they had the previous year. Ashley sold his Rocky Mountain Fur Company to Jedediah Smith, William Sublette and David Jackson.

A Hawkin 58 caliber rifle - could take down a buffalo

Mountain Men and the Rendezvous

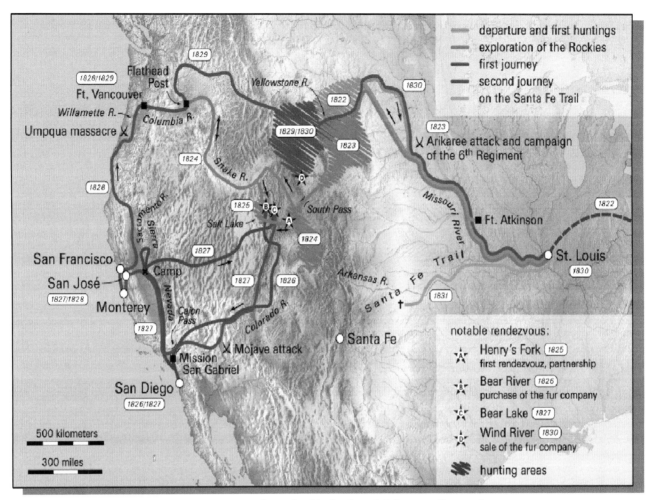

Map of Jedediah Smith's explorations
Courtesy of Maximilian Dörrbecker, Wikipedia

Rough going

Smith left his partners and headed out south and west of Great Salt Lake, by way of the Mohave Desert and the San Bernardino Mountains. When he was out of supplies, he headed for the San Gabriel Mission.

Politically, the Spanish in California mistook Smith's reasons for being there and suspected that he was involved in some sort of claims for the United States. Finding beaver aplenty in the valley of the San Joaquin River, he was able to resupply his group to cross back over the Sierra Nevada.

They had 1,500 pounds of beaver that they had to cache as they could not get through on the American River route. Deep snow made it impossible. They were forced to turn back. In the end, it was a most terrible trip.

In the spring, three men and seven horses took three weeks to cross through Ebbetts Pass. They were forced to eat some of their horses and they were desperate for water. When Robert Evans gave out and gave up, two men continued on. When they finally found water, Jedediah

Smith party crossing the terrible desert

brought some back to Evans, who did recover. Passing by the southern end of the Great Salt Lake, they turned northward to Cache Valley and then on to Bear Lake to the rendezvous.

As can be imagined, they were very well-received – everyone had thought that they had been lost for good. Naturally, it was a genuinely pleasant surprise to see them, causing much merriment among their friends.

At the end of summer, 1827, they headed back again to California, retracing their route. This time, you can be sure that Robert Evans most definitely did not go with them.

Coming down the south side of Utah Lake, they came on to the Colorado River. Smith and half of his men had just crossed the river when Mojave Indians attacked and killed 10 of the men who had not yet crossed the river. When the Indians came after Smith's group, they were fought off and soon gave up. Smith's men made it to the San Gabriel Mission, but misunderstandings of a political nature with the Mexican authorities landed Smith in jail for three weeks.

Smith beholds the Pacific

After wintering in the Sacramento Valley, they returned from California, trapping the Yuba, the Feather and the Sacramento River, and then northwest to the Trinity River, South Fork, and Klamath Rivers. A month later, they finally beheld the Pacific Ocean.

Coming up the Rogue River in late summer, the group rescued a 10-year-old boy from the Willamette Valley. Later, they crossed the

Umpqua River, then Smith's River, trading for beaver and sea otter skins.

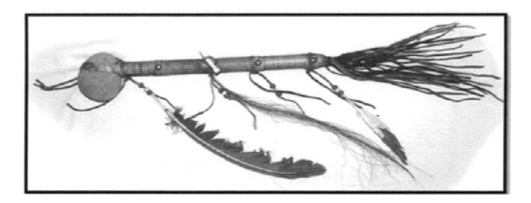

Tomahawk

While Smith and two others were out looking for possible travel routes, one of the men innocently let a group of Indians into camp who massacred all but one man, Arthur Black. When Jedediah and his companions returned, the Indians fired on them, but, it being apparent that everyone was dead, they soon left. Jedediah and his men had escaped.

Strength in numbers

Arthur Black thought he was the only one to survive when he got to Fort Vancouver, but three days later, Smith and the two others came into the fort. Hudson's Bay Company didn't appreciate such goings on in their trapping area, so they determined to immediately retaliate and recover Smith's furs. Hudson's Bay bought the beaver from Smith for $2,500.

After a four-month stay at the fort, Jedediah made his way back to his partner, David Jackson. They missed the 1829 rendezvous at the Popo Agie, but later met up with partner William Sublette at Pierre's Hole. They then split up in three directions. Sublette brought the furs to St. Louis; Jackson trapped the Snake River; Smith went into Blackfoot land with Jim Bridger. At the next rendezvous at Popo Agie, the partners sold out to five men: Tom Fitzpatrick, Milton Sublette, Jim Bridger, Fraeb and Gervais, the founders of the Rocky Mountain Fur Company.

Jedediah went again to California with 74 men. At one point in their journey, he went out looking for water – and was never seen again. It is believed that he was killed by Comanche Indians on the Santa Fe Trail in May 1831.

Liz Sartori

Chapter 13

Thomas Fitzpatrick – "White-Hair"

Thomas Fitzpatrick was an able mountain man. He had started at the bottom and worked in all parts of the enterprise. Having been an Indian agent, he understood much that others perhaps missed.

Fitzpatrick was born in Ireland in 1799 and came to America at age 16. He had been educated and was well-spoken and well-written. He had joined Ashley's young men and went up the Missouri with him. Tom partnered with Jedediah Smith and the two went overland to Wyoming, wintering near the Crows in the Wind River Valley. They crossed South Pass and trapped in the Green River Valley.

A plan pays off

Their trapping being successful, Fitzpatrick carried the furs back while

Smith kept trapping. Fitzpatrick was using a bull boat, but he ran into difficulties, abandoned the boat and cached his furs.

Bull boats, painting by Karl Bodmer (1809–1893)

Continuing on east on foot, he met Ashley with supplies. Fitzpatrick guided his old "boss" to the Green River, where they chose the site for the July rendezvous. He led a small party up Henry's Fork of the Green River where streams ran north from the Uinta Mountains. The trapping season had been successful, with 140 pelts from Fitzpatrick's group.

Near Great Salt Lake, Fitzpatrick, Jim Bridger, and Jim Beckwourth got involved in a fracas with Indians. The Indians made off with some of their horses. To deal with this affront, the men got up a plan: Fitzpatrick's group came directly at the Indians while Bridger ran off the horses. The trappers got all their horses back – and 40 more, besides! In the fighting, six Indians were killed, but all the trappers got off unscathed.

Rendezvous

Fitzpatrick partnered with William Sublette in 1826-27, and was at the Bear Lake Rendezvous in 1827 and 1828. Then Tom went with David Jackson to Flathead country, but Hudson's Bay Company was already there and had thoroughly taken over. They did meet Jedediah Smith there.

In 1829, Fitzpatrick rode to meet William Sublette with his supply caravan. The parties met on the Popo Agie branch of the Wind River and had a rendezvous in July. Thomas then guided Sublette westward to a meeting with his partners, Jackson and Smith, at Pierre's Hole. There they held a second rendezvous.

Courageous action

In the fall, Tom and Sublette went on a trapping tour to the headwaters of the Missouri. There, hostile Blackfeet tried to run off the trappers' herd of horses. With instant courage, Tom jumped on his horse; others followed, and they rode around the camp containing their herd. No fewer than two horses were shot right out from under Fitzpatrick.

At the rendezvous in 1830, they met William Sublette with all the supplies. While they were all together, with no apparent advance planning, they unexpectedly bought Smith, Jackson, and Sublette's mountain fur interests. The five new owners were Thomas Fitzpatrick, Jim Bridger, Milton Sublette (William's brother), Henry Fraeb, and Jean Gervais.

As new owners, they got to work. Fraeb and Gervais led 33 men up to the Snake River area. Fitzpatrick and two others led their group of 80 into Blackfoot country. They worked the Powder River and spent a cold winter on the Yellowstone. Fitzpatrick took off to get supplies, but since Smith, Jackson, and Sublette were already on their way to New Mexico, he had to go with them for their mutual protection. Because of the detour to New Mexico, Tom returned late to outfit at the rendezvous, giving his goods to Fraeb and then rushed back to the Missouri to provide for *next* year's supplies.

"White-Hair"

While Fitzpatrick had been gone, the American Fur Company men had been harassing his men, giving them a hard time because the Rocky Mountain Fur Company was trapping roughly the same ground. To top it off, Tom had a bad encounter with some Gros Ventres Indians and lost his horse, his gun, and his equipment. Much to his relief, he was rescued by two men who had come searching for him. After this experience, his hair turned grey overnight and which earned him the name "White-Hair" ever afterwards.

Trading Post, 1898 painting by C. M. Russell

On the brighter side, supplies had arrived and they held one of the biggest of all the sixteen rendezvous that were ever held by mountain men. Gathered there were Rocky Mountain fur men, independent trappers and friendly Indians.

Battle at Pierre's Hole

It was right after this great rendezvous that a frightful battle took place at Pierre's Hole. A valley nestled in the Teton Mountain Range in what is now eastern Idaho, Pierre's Hole was named after a French trapper who had been killed by Indians in 1828.

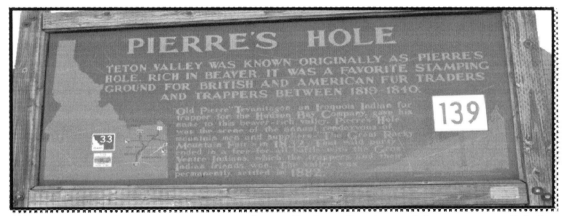

Plaque marking 1832 Pierre's Hole Battle Area Site, eastern Idaho

The hostile Gros Ventres had built a breastwork, a log fortification, in the swampy willows nearby. The trappers and their allies drove the Gros Ventres into the woods and William Sublette was wounded early in the attack on the fortification. They fought until dark with no clear victor.

The next morning, the trappers and the friendlies rushed the breastwork, but the hostiles had disappeared, leaving behind a number of dead warriors and thirty dead horses. Five of the trappers had been killed and seven of the friendlies. A dozen had been wounded in the fierce battle. In this jungle of willows, Fitzpatrick had been the commander.

But it was not a fighting force organized in the typical pattern - the trappers were all used to thinking as individuals.

In the fall of 1832, Tom Fitzpatrick and Jim Bridger led their party to Clark's Fork on the Missouri. American Fur Company men were there, also and both groups ended up fighting with the Blackfeet. The leader of the other group, Vanderburg, was killed.

Competitive practices

After wintering on the Salmon River, the trappers netted 40 packs of fur in their spring trapping.

Summer rendezvous came and arrangements were made to deliver the furs. Fitzpatrick and his group – over 20 trappers - went on to the Powder River. There, the Crows, instigated by the American Fur trappers, robbed them. Bad luck dogged Fitzpatrick and the competition between the fur companies led to competition also in the delivery of supplies.

Fitzpatrick's men bought from the supplies that had arrived earlier to the rendezvous, leaving Wyeth, who had arrived a little later, with his goods unsold. Ever enterprising, Wyeth built Fort Hall and was able to sell his supplies from there.

Fitzpatrick, Bridger and Milton Sublette joined Fontenelle and Drips, forming Fontenelle, Fitzpatrick, and Company. Bridger and Drips stayed in the mountains while Fitzpatrick and Fontenelle took their furs on to St. Louis.

Guide
Later on, Tom Fitzpatrick and his partners bought Fort William on the

Laramie River from William Sublette and Robert Campbell. Fitzpatrick became involved in guiding the Marcus Whitman/Spalding missionary party to Oregon, while still trying to work another trip into the mountains.

The American Fur Company bought them out, including the fort, and Tom Fitzpatrick went back to the business of trapping and delivering furs. A couple of years went by in which the details of his adventures are lost, though his name is often mentioned as working in the trapping enterprise.

The fur trade was fading out, giving Tom Fitzpatrick an opportunity to guide a large party over the Oregon Trail, even rescuing them from a buffalo stampede. One person on the trip said they would *never* have made it without Fitzpatrick's able help. The members of another emigrant party whom he guided to Fort Hall were equally impressed and grateful, praising his skill with the Indians and his keen knowledge of the terrain.

Immigrants heading west; painting by Albert Bierstadt

Two groups within the Oregon-bound group, lead by Bartleson and Bidwell, wanted to split off and go to California. Fitzpatrick told them frankly that he had no information on the California route and he strongly recommended that they seek out Joseph Walker, who was familiar with the route, having guided John C. Fremont throughout this vast region.

When the leaders of the groups could not find Walker, they went it alone. They were soon to realize the folly of going without a guide. Their journey was long and terrible. Because of the route they had chosen, they were forced to abandon their wagons, packing everything onto their over-burdened horses and mules. This trying journey stretched out into a harrowing six-month ordeal. We see the wisdom of guides at this time in our history.

Army guide and Indian agent

Fitzpatrick also guided John Charles Fremont's second and longest trip. He then guided with Kearney and with the army, followed by a stint with the army outfit of James Abert. The Mexican war began in 1846 and Tom played a key role in guiding the army, which was trying to catch traders who were undermining their efforts by selling guns to the Mexicans.

Later still, Kit Carson took Tom's place with the army while Tom delivered dispatches to Washington.

It was while he was in Washington that Fitzpatrick discovered that he had been appointed to be Indian agent in the Upper Platte and Arkansas River region. He taught and counseled with the Cheyennes, and his work with seven or more Indian tribes gave rise to a large western council

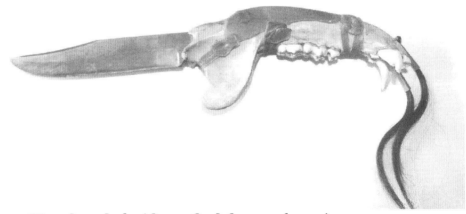
Fort Laramie Treaty 1851, an early draft

that lead up to the Fort Laramie Treaty of 1851.

Thomas Fitzpatrick, fur trapper, guide, explorer, and Indian agent, died in Washington from pneumonia February 7, 1854, leaving a wife and two children.

Handmade knife crafted from a bear jaw

Liz Sartori

Kit Carson - Trapper, Army Scout, Guide, Indian Fighter, Soldier

Kit Carson was one of the most well-known of the mountain men in his day and became somewhat of a national hero. This status was probably conferred on him because of his role as an Indian agent, or perhaps because, on two occasions, he guided the famous John C. Fremont, taking him into the Rocky Mountains.

Kit runs away

Kit Carson, born Christopher Carson, was only 9 years old in 1818 when his father died. His mother soon remarried. As was the custom in those days, when he was 14, Kit went to work in a saddle shop to learn a trade. He didn't like it at all and at 16 ran away on a wagon train to Santa Fe.

On the wagon train, he spent time with Matthew Kinkead, who had been a friend of his father's, a trapper with two seasons of experience under his belt.

Kit was restless and switched to another wagon train as a teamster. After spending some time in Taos, he worked as an interpreter for a merchant in Chihuahua. Switching tracks again, he joined up as a teamster at a copper mine.

Trapping adventures

The next year, Kit tried his hand as a trapper in Arizona and learned all he could. We don't hear about many southwestern fur trappers – a shorter season, no doubt.

Signing up with Thomas Fitzpatrick, he began 10 years of trapping in the Rockies, chalking up scores of adventures. The first year, their horses were stolen and, after they managed to get them back, he and his mates attacked the Comanche village, just for fun. On one memorable occasion, Kit tangled with a grizzly bear. Another time, the story goes, with **two** grizzlies.

The formidable grizzly bear

Once Kit and his mates were attacked by 200 Comanches and, forting down behind their mules, they killed 42 Indians and then slipped away into the night. The next time they were attacked, they thought there were only two Indians – instead, there were 60! The attack turned into a retreat and back to camp they sped. Later Kit and his friends fought Blackfeet in Crow territory.

Hunter at $1 a day

Kit hunted Brown's Hole, staying at Fort Davy Crockett on the Green River. In 1840, he sold all his furs to Antoine Robidoux at Fort Uintah. Then, in 1841, Kit hunted the spring hunt in Utah. Fur trapping was coming to an end, with fur prices sinking lower and lower.

By this time, Kit's wife had died and he had two children to support, so he had to change his free-wheeling style. With Bill Williams and Colorado Mitchell, Kit headed to Bent's Old Fort on the Arkansas River and became a hunter for wages - $1 a day.

The following year, thinking of his children, Carson remarried, this time to a young sister of Charles Bent.

Carson met Lieutenant Fremont at the beginning of Fremont's western explorations when he was 32 years old and Fremont was 28. Kit Carson did well as a guide. He had found a way to stay in his beloved west.

About the arrival of the exploring party in a green area in the Nevada desert, Carson waxed poetic.

> Our adventures in the desert were eventually terminated by our arrival at "Las Vegas de Santa Clara", and a pleasant thing it was to look once more upon green grass and sweet water, and to reflect that the dreariest part of our journey lay behind us, so that the sands and tornados of the Great Basin would weary our animals no more... The noise of running water, the large grassy meadows from which the spot takes its name, and the green hills which circle it round – all seem to captivate the eye and please the senses of the well-worn "voyageur".   – Kit Carson

Gone for a soldier

Still later, Carson was a soldier in the Mexican War. He was a guide in the war and became a currier to President Polk in Washington, while still remaining an Indian fighter. Carson left Los Angeles with 15 European-Americans and 6 Delaware Indians, vowing to make the trip in 60 days. The party met up with Tom Fitzpatrick and Joe Walker, who had also guided for John C. Fremont. Fremont always preferred Kit Carson, however.

Kit Carson drove 6,500 sheep from New Mexico to California

Turning to another enterprise, Kit and a fellow by the name of Maxwell drove 6,500 sheep from Taos, New Mexico to California and came away with a good bit of profit. Having bought the sheep for 50 cents a head, they managed to sell them for $5.50 apiece. According to one version of the story, there was more than one herd of sheep and many more men making the journey with them.

Sympathetic Indian agent

Kit Carson became an Indian agent in New Mexico and served well in that office. He did the best he could to carry out government orders, but he did have a sympathetic understanding of the Indians, a quality that they appreciated.

Later years

During the Civil War, Kit was a Colonel in the first New Mexico volunteers. He was brevet Brigadier-General when he took command of Fort Garland in Colorado.

Kit Carson's biographers admired his integrity and his extraordinary courage, but Kit remained a modest man. Lieutenant Fremont admired his fine horsemanship. He smoked a pipe, but, uncharacteristic of a mountain man, he never drank alcohol.

A fall from a horse coupled with a subsequent illness troubled his final years. Carson died in 1868, just three years after the Civil War had ended.

Liz Sartori

Chapter 15

Jim Baker - On the Edge

Jim Baker lived a long life - 80 years - and was a most colorful mountain man. He wore Indian clothing and learned their customs, over time marrying six Indian squaws. One wife was the daughter of Chief Washakie of the Shoshones, and another was the daughter of a Cherokee chief.

Of Scotch-Irish descent, Jim Baker was born in Illinois, but at an early age, he *walked* from his home to St. Louis, Missouri, and there met Jim Bridger, an event that would forever change his life.

In May, 1839, Baker joined a trapping expedition, traveling up the Missouri River to Kansas City on an old steamer, and thence on to Grande Island. His party travelled in keelboats. They went on down the

Medicine Bow River, then the Laramie River to the Sweetwater and on to Fort Bonneville (near present-day Daniel, Wyoming).

Keelboat on the river

Baker spent 1838 and 1839 trapping in the Wind River Mountains, in what is now Wyoming, returning home to Illinois in 1840.

The next year, Baker set out on another journey to the Rocky Mountains. He joined Jim Bridger at his camp at Henry's Fork of the Snake River. Bridger was worried about his trapper friend, Henry Fraeb (also spelled Frappe and Frap in some sources), who had gone out trapping from the camp and hadn't returned, so he sent Jim Baker and several other men out to look for Fraeb's party.

In their search, they inadvertently stumbled upon - and took part in - what was to become the famous battle with the Sioux, Cheyenne, and Arapaho at Bastion Mountain, later renamed Battle Mountain. Fraeb was killed early in the battle, leaving Jim Bridger, at only 21 years of age, in charge of the rest of the 35 trappers. After the Indians finally retreated, Baker and the other survivors struggled back to Bridger's camp.

After about 6 years of trapping and spending some of this time with "friendlies" (friendly Indian groups), Baker settled for a short time in Salt Lake City, where he became a government scout and guide. He already had the ability to speak and understand Shoshone and could sign with the Arapaho.

Jim Baker had his finger in many pies, making for a colorful and varied life. In 1859, Jim Baker homesteaded near Denver at what is now 53rd and Tennyson Street. He tried his hand as the owner of a toll bridge and it seems that he owned the very first coal mine in Colorado. During this period, Baker also became a captain in the Colorado militia.

In 1873, Baker left Colorado and went to ranching in Savory, Wyoming. Three of his daughters, Isabel, Madeline, and Jennie, lived with him in his last location in Savory. They helped him build a three-story cabin out of the local cottonwood trees. The third floor had a special purpose - a look-out post for spotting potential Indian enemies. Later, when such dangers were past, the third story was removed.

It seems that Jim Baker couldn't stay put very long, or perhaps he was in great demand, but just two years later, in 1875, he was off again, scouting under George Custer during the historic fight with the Sioux at Rosebud, in the Black Hills. Then again, in 1881, Baker served under General Thornburg against the Utes at the battle of the Meeker Massacre, which rocked the whole country and lead to the forcible removal of the Ute people to Utah.

After having traveled from Missouri to Oregon, from California to Kansas Territory, from Salt Lake and over the Rocky Mountains, Jim

Baker died at his cabin in Savory, Wyoming on May 15, 1898, after a restless and eventful life.

Even Baker's cabin traveled a lot! It was removed to Frontier Park in Cheyenne, Wyoming in 1917, and then returned to Savory, Wyoming in 1976. It now stands in the Little Snake River Museum. Its reconstruction was directed by Paul McAllister, a great grandson of Baker's who lives in Wyoming.

Jim Baker lies in a little cemetery overlooking his beloved Snake River Valley.

Baker Cabin, Frontier Park, Cheyenne, July 1920.
Photo by Lt. Flag A. Drewry, courtesy of Mary Carol Schrupp

Scout Charles Stobie, D.C. Oakes, Indian Agent, with Jim Baker
Courtesy Colorado Historical Society, Denver

Liz Sartori

Jim Beckwourth – A Man for All Seasons

A mulatto trapper, Jim Beckwourth lived to the age of 69. He was born into slavery in Virginia, but spent all of his adult life in the west. Like many others, he came to the Rocky Mountains with Ashley as a trapper. Later, Beckwourth went to live with the Crows and adopted their ways, choosing for himself multiple Indian wives.

Beckwourth spent time as a guide for Stephen Kearney during the Mexican War and, after many adventuresome and entrepreneurial experiences, he went back to live among the Crows until his death.

Good news, bad news

Jim Beckwourth was born into slavery. That's the bad news. The good news is that his father and master (translate - owner) freed him at early age and gave him the opportunity to learn a trade. He was apprenticed to a blacksmith, a trade that, though he learned it well, didn't suit his adventurous personality

After having experienced many adventures, Beckwourth told his life story to an itinerant justice of the peace named Thomas Bonner, who wrote it all down. The resulting book about his life as a trapper and scout, and as a chief among the Crow tribe, was published in 1856 in London. Four years later, it was translated into French and published in France.

CHAPTER XXX.

Departure for the Mountains.—Severe Sickness on the Way.—Arrival at Bent's Fort.—Arrival at Sublet's Fort.—Interview with the Cheyennes.—Difficulty with a Sioux Warrior.—His Death.—Successful Trade opened with various Tribes.—Incidents 422

CHAPTER XXXI.

Invitation to visit the Outlaws.—Interview with "the Elk that Calls."—Profitable Trade with the Outlaws.—Return to the Post.—Great Alarm among the Traders.—Five Horses killed at the Fort.—Flight from the Siouxs.—Safe arrival at the Fort.—Trade with the Arrapa-hos.—Attacked by a Cheyenne Warrior.—Peace restored... 438

CHAPTER XXXII.

First Trip to New Mexico.—Return to the Indians with Goods.—Success in Trade.—Enter into Business in St. Fernandez.—Get Married.—Return to the Indians.—The fortunate Speculation.—Proceed to California with Goods 456

CHAPTER XXXIII.

The Californian Revolution.—Rifle Corps.—Position of the two Armies.—Colonel Sutter.—Cannonade.—Flight of Sutter.—His Return.—Trial and subsequent Release 466

CHAPTER XXXIV.

Affairs at Santa Fé.—Insurrection at Taos.—Discovery of the Plot.—Battle at the Cañon.—Battles at Lambida, at Pueblo, and at Taos.

Excerpt from Table of Contents of Beckwourth's book: "The Life and Adventures of James P. Beckwourth, Mountaineer, Scout, and Pioneer, and Chief of the Crow Nation of Indians"

Beckwourth's book is now considered a valuable piece of social history and, in the 1960's, Beckwourth was acknowledged as an early African American pioneer. In children's literature and in textbooks, this multi-faceted man is featured as a role model.

It appears very significant for his times (born in 1798 or 1800) that his father (of English and Irish nobility named Beckworth) acknowledged him as his son. He freed young James by manumission, or deed of emancipation, in 1824, '25, and '26. James Beckwourth raised all of his slave-wife's 13 children. Young James was her third child.

As a young man, after receiving some schooling and finishing a blacksmith apprenticeship at age 19, Beckwourth (his choice for spelling his name) joined Ashley's group as a wrangler, caring for the horses. Later he became an important trapper and mountain man.

> Beckwourth was becoming restless because he wasn't rich and famous enough, saying:
> "I have encountered savage beasts and wild men...and what have I to show for so much wasted energy, and such a catalogue of ruthless deeds?"

There are two accounts of his subsequent time among the Crow Indian tribe. Jim himself said the Crows thought he was a lost son of the Crow chief. Other accounts say that he was among the Crows as part of a plan of the Rocky Mountain Fur Company to help open trade possibilities with that tribe.

Still later, Beckwourth left the rocky Mountain Fur Company and sold his furs to John Jacob Astor's Company.

Beckwourth worked for the U.S. Army as a wagon-master in the baggage division during the Second Seminole War in Florida. Then, from 1838 to 1848, he was an Indian trader to the Cheyenne on the Arkansas River, working out of Fort Vasquez, Colorado near Platteville.

After this, he worked at Fort Bent on the Arkansas River in the Bent and St. Vrain Company, followed by a short stint as an independent trader.

With partners, Beckwourth began a trading post in Colorado which later became the center of Pueblo, Colorado. In 1848 we find Jim in Sonoma, California as a storeowner during the gold rush. He sold out and headed up to Sacramento to be a professional card player in the boomtown of that time.

Beckwourth appears to have jumped from one interesting thing to another, and in 1850 we find him in the Sierra Nevada Mountains discovering what was later named Beckwourth Pass, one of the lowest crossings of the Sierra Nevadas.

The story goes, he made a deal with the folks of Marysville to vastly improve an Indian trail, transforming it into what became the Beckwourth Trail. But Marysville couldn't afford to pay him for his work, so they renamed a park for him , Beckwourth Riverfront Park.

The trail started at Pyramid Lake and the Truckee Meadows, went up through the pass, along a ridge between two forks of the Feather River, and down into Northern California's gold fields at Marysville.

One very important feature of this trail is that travelers were spared 150 miles they would have had to travel on other routes, *including the trip up through Donner's Pass.* Significantly, the Western Pacific Railroad later used this same crossing of the Sierra Nevada Mountains.

In the period from 1850 to 1859, Beckwourth began ranching. He had a ranch, a trading post, and a hotel in the Sierra Valley, which together made up the beginnings of Beckwourth, California. It was during this period when he told his life story to Thomas Bonner.

Briefly, we follow Beckwourth to Missouri and thence on to Denver, Colorado as a store-keeper and local agent for Indian affairs.

In 1859, Beckwourth began scouting for Colonel John M. Chivington of the Third Colorado Volunteers for their campaign against the Cheyenne and Arapahoe. It was at this time that the terrible Sand Creek Massacre occurred. 160 families of Native Americans - men, women, and children – were attacked by the military, and the military had even sported an American flag to show a friendly face.

Understandably, there were repercussions and fall-out over this incident. Beckwourth returned to trapping.

Jim Beckwourth was in his late 60's when he began to get nosebleeds; some believe these were caused by hypertension. He returned to his Crow people and died among them October 29, 1866 of an unstoppable nose-bleed.

Liz Sartori

Chapter 17

John Colter – Distance Runner

A trapper and an explorer, John Colter filled his 38 years of life to the brim. He was a member of the Louis and Clark Expedition and was quickly became known as their best game hunter.

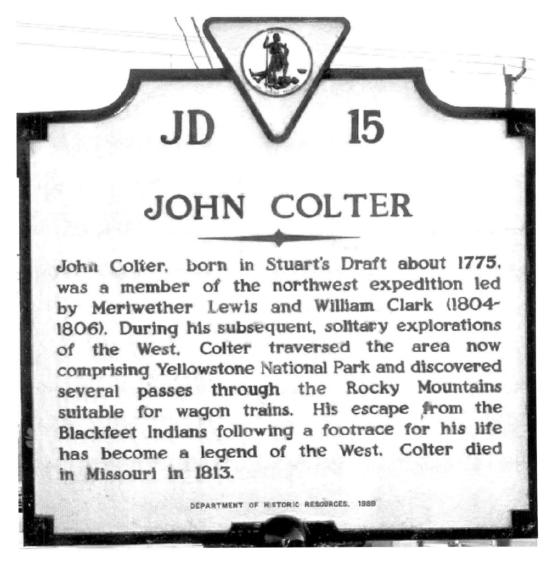

Sign in Stuart's Draft, Virginia commemorating Jim Colter

On that expedition, Colter was one of a small group that had the privilege of going all the way to the shores of the Pacific Ocean and then up the coast to present-day Washington.

After thousands of miles of travel, in 1806 they came to the Mandan Indian villages in present-day North Dakota. Colter was allowed to muster out early to enable him to lead Forest Hancock and Joseph Dickson, two frontiersmen who wanted to search for furs in the upper Missouri. Back he went to the region that the Lewis and Clark party had just explored.

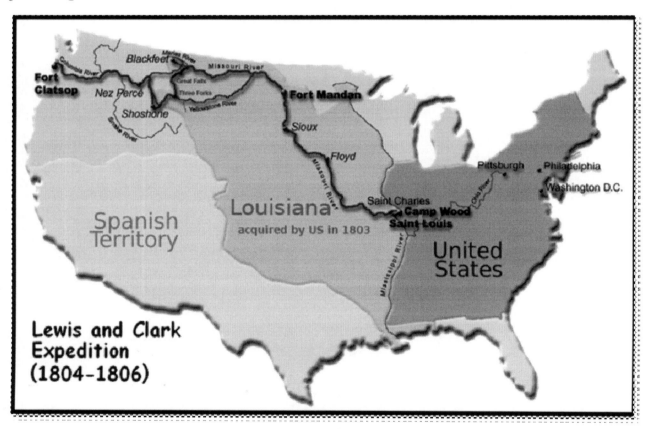

John Colter went with the expedition all the way to the Pacific
Map courtesy of EncMstr, Urban

After reaching the three forks of the Gallatin River, Jefferson River, and Madison River they partnered for two months. When Jim Colter was returning, he chanced to cross paths with Manuel Lisa who was leading a party towards the Rocky Mountains. Colter joined them and headed west again, even though he was only a week's journey from St. Louis.

Where the Yellowstone and Bighorn Rivers meet, he helped build Fort Raymond. From there, he was sent out to interest the Crows in fur trade. Covering a lot of ground, he saw the Grand Teton Range of mountains, the first white person to see this awe-inspiring range. When he described the sights he had beheld in Yellowstone, he couldn't get folks to believe that he had seen what he had seen.

Long-distance runner

Colter is best known for his "run" from the Blackfeet Indians. Here's how that happened. Colter was trapping beaver in Montana with John Potts, when a large group of Blackfeet Indians attacked them. Potts was killed and they made Colter run from them, naked, with a 400-yard start. And run he did - a large party chasing him intent on killing him - plenty motivated!

Managing somehow to stay ahead of his pursuers, Colter suddenly flung out his arms, surprising the last brave who was following close behind him. Snatching the lance from the startled and exhausted Indian, Colter swiftly killed him. Full of courage, he even took the Indian's blanket!

The cleverly designed beaver lodge has ample air space within

Colter dragged himself to the Madison River, and, not trusting that he was safe even then, hid inside a beaver lodge for the night.

Despite exhaustion, he then walked for eleven days, reaching the nearest trading outpost on the Little Bighorn in a week's time.

Later, Colter helped build another fort at Three Forks, Montana.

Colter often explored alone. On one memorable occasion, he returned to the fort with his fur pelts to discover that two of his partners had been killed. Dismayed, he returned to St. Louis.

With his wife Sallie, Colter went back to live in Missouri where they bought some land and went to farming. He was able to meet again with William Clark and give him detailed reports of his explorations since their last meeting over 6 years earlier.

During the War of 1812, Colter fought with Nathan Boone's Rangers.

It is not entirely certain whether John Colter died in May 1812, or November 1813. The best guess was a sudden illness on top of a case of jaundice.

Jim Bridger - Survivor

Jim Bridger was a survivor. Indeed, he outlived nearly all the other mountain men. When he finally died in 1881, he was 69 years old.

Bridger was an avid explorer, a guide for the military, and a respected guide for emigrants. Jim was known for his tale tales of mountain adventure and the Indians. Even when the fur trade era was ending, Bridger figured out ways to allow him to continue living in the mountains.

Jim Bridger is perhaps best known for his encounter at Fort Bridger with Brigham Young and the Mormon pioneers. History records that Bridger expressed strong doubt that the Mormons could survive in the region. Perhaps because he didn't want competition for his fort and wanted the Mormons to move on to California, he allegedly made the remark, "I'd give $1,000 for the first bushel of corn grown in the Salt Lake Valley!"

A hard worker

As a youth, Jim learned to work hard. By the time he was 14 years old he was an orphan with a little sister. He worked on a flat boat on the big river, then apprenticed to a blacksmith. He met people of all sorts and eagerly learned many vital things from them. He had also heard of some of the early mountain men like Manuel Lisa, John Colter, and the Chouteau family of trappers and had even seen some of these men in St. Louis, where Jim lived and worked.

An ad placed by William H. Ashley appeared in the newspaper. It called for trappers who would be willing to follow the Missouri River to its source.

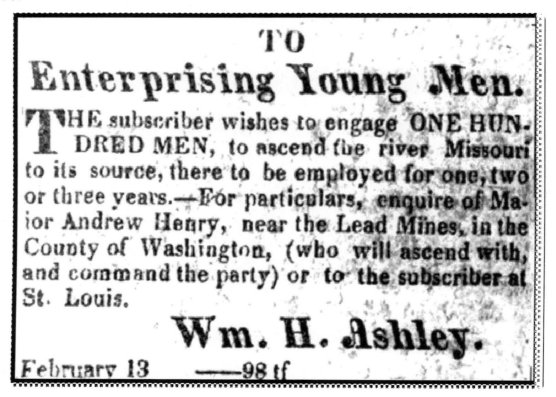

Famous ad placed by Ashley in St. Louis newspaper in 1820

The men who responded to this advertisement became known as "Ashley's Hundred." And Jim Bridger was quick to respond to the ad. "And the rest," as they say, "is history."

Two keelboats started down the river, led by Ashley and Major Andrew Henry. Jim found himself on the riverbank addressing Major Andrew Henry, eager to sign on. Henry knew Jim from the blacksmith shop, liked his work ethic and clean rifle, and hired him right on the spot.

It was Andrew who determined to hire white trappers and hold camps to trap beaver so no place would be trapped out as it had been around the established posts. On the warmer off seasons, they could hunt new locations on the rivers and scout out new rivers.

Bridger was with Andrew Henry for his first major Indian fight with the 'Rees (Arikara Indians). Hugh Glass, an old trapper had gone on ahead a little and had been attacked by a mother bear. He had gotten so chewed up that no one expected he could possibly live. When it was clear that the injured trapper could not go on, Jim and a fellow named Fitzgerald stayed with him. After three days with no improvement for Glass, the men felt they needed to catch up with their group. Convinced that there was no way in the world for Glass to recover, they left him in the middle of the night, taking all his plunder.

When they rejoined their group, they told the others that Hugh Glass was dead because it didn't seem to matter one way or the other. They split into groups and trapped beaver, each man setting his own traps in the rivers.

A ghost appears

In January, they went back to the fort on the Big Horn. Jim thought about Hugh Glass often, and worried over his final days, even imagining his final moments. One night, Glass miraculously showed up and Jim thought he was a ghost. The "ghost" grabbed his arm and commanded him to speak before he shot him. At that moment, Andrew arrived, along knew blacksmithing, supply gathering, leadership, and he knew a dozen Indian languages. (He also knew English, French, and Spanish.) He went at it. with everyone else in the group, and stopped the action. He "invited" Jim and Hugh to his quarters.

Glass told his story, a gruesome tale of waking and finding himself alone and defenseless. Realizing he had been abandoned by his caretakers, anger burned inside him. An unshakable determination was born, a burning determination to make it and to make Bridger and Fitzgerald pay. He had crawled back to the fort – a journey of 200 miles!

With uncanny luck, Hugh Glass had come upon a partly eaten buffalo calf carcass temporarily left by the wolves. Better nourished and revived from the meat, he was able to follow a river, even getting a short ride on a boat. He was given some plunder from the Indians and finally had drug himself in to the fort.

Later, Glass left the fort alone with knife, rifle, flint and steel, thinking obsessively about catching up with Fitzgerald.

Jim Bridger had learned his lesson and ever after looked out for everyone he had anything to do with. In fact, he became known for his great qualities of courage and generosity.

Mountain Men and the Rendezvous

Shot in the back

Jim Bridger decided to become a free trapper with no booshway (boss). After more adventures trapping, year after year, Jim's character became well-known. Eight years after signing on with Major Andrews, Jim became a booshway, himself, for the Rocky Mountain Fur Company.

The richer American Fur Company came after him to cash in on what he had, but Bridger's group headed out to Pierre's Hole. Things did not go well there and a battle between the trappers and the Gros Ventres Indians ensued. Bridger was even shot in the back and the arrow head was left where it had lodged. Later, the Crows stole their horses and it was a great deal of trouble to get replacements.

In the summer of 1835, the rendezvous was held at Green River, where there was a group of Indians and two hundred trappers. Somehow, it seemed the time was right to get that old arrowhead out, what with Dr. Marcus Whitman and Dr. Samuel Parker right there. Jim had been carrying around that arrowhead inside him for three years. And now - it was gone!

At age thirty, Bridger took a wife. "Trapping a squaw", was what the Indians called it.

By then, the fur-trapping years had pretty much come to a close. Jim tried heading back to St. Louis, but he couldn't stand the shoes, the clothes, just generally being hemmed in, and decided to head for the mountains again.

He became a scout for the military for $10 a day – and sometimes they didn't take his advice, often to their later regret.

Staying in the Mountains

Finally, Jim Bridger did find a way to stay in the mountains - he built his own fort, Fort Bridger. He knew the Indians; he knew sign language. He

When finished, the fort had a store; there was trading and selling of horses, mules and buffalo robes, deerskins, clay pipes, tobacco, whisky, buckskin clothing. Jim's his partner Vasquez looked after this end of the bustling fort, while Jim advised travelers, charted trails, and welcomed a stream of visitors. As a sideline, he also ran the forge.

Fort Bridger in its active days

Sad News

Many do not know what a family man Jim Bridger was. His wife had died at the fort after a difficult childbirth. A mourning Jim named his baby girl Virginia. There was no one to give his baby milk, so, when Jim's cow went dry, he went out every day and brought in a buffalo's.

udder. Virginia grew well and happy. In time, Jim had three Indian wives and outlived them all. One cold winter afternoon in 1847, with snow piled high around the stockade, some men came riding into the fort. Bridger could make out his old friend Joe Meek and greeted him warmly.

No sound came from Meek. Grasping Joe's his hand warmly, Jim hollered, "Hi, Ol' Hoss!" Still no reply from Joe. Jim knew there was trouble.

Sculpture of Jim Bridger

Filled with sorrow, Joe Meek told Jim about the massacre at the Whitman mission by the Cayuse Indians. Finally it all came tumbling out - Joe's daughter had been killed, along with the rest. Jim's daughter

Mary Ann, who had also been living at the Whitman mission, was missing, taken away by the Indians. Jim knew that he'd never see her again in this life.

After this tragedy, Jim took the rest of his little family to Kansas to keep them safe ever after.

John Johnson – "Liver-Eating Johnson"

John Johnson was a unique mountain man in several ways. He nursed a vendetta against the Crow Indians because some Crows killed his wife, a Flathead Indian. He came late on the scene of the fur trapping business. He fought in the Civil War - at age 41 – joining up on the Union side in February of 1864, for the last year, which officially ended in April of 1865. Later in life, he was a highly respected sheriff. Although he was known by many nick names, he was best known as "Jeremiah Johnson".

Del Gue, a trapper who had spent considerable time with Johnson, related much of John Johnson's story to "White Eye", J.F. Anderson.

> In 1847, Johnson's wife, a member of the Flathead tribe, was killed by the Crow, which prompted Johnson to pursue a vendetta against the entire tribe. Legend says that he would kill, then cut out and eat the liver of each Crow brave he came across. This was an insult to the Crow, who believed the liver to be vital for the journey into the afterlife. In any case, he eventually became known as "Liver-Eating Johnson".

Johnson's greatest activity occurred after the fur trapping business was on the wane. The last official rendezvous was held in 1840 and Johnson came into the fur trapping business in 1843, as a young man, living until 1900. Having a life that long, when one lives in constantly dangerous circumstances, is unique in itself.

Many mountain men

There were hundreds of fur trappers and mountain men, but the ones we read about are relatively few. Those well-known few had promoters who wrote about them, or they promoted themselves. John Johnson knew a great many of the mountain men and we know he knew them, because his story has been written and these men are mentioned in it, even though their own stories were not written down in detail.

Names come up in Johnson's story such as Old John Hatcher, who befriended and taught him the trapping trade – and how to keep his hair; Bill Williams, "Bear Claw" Chris Lapp, who made polished claw necklaces taken from grizzly bears and who was killed later by the

Blackfoot Indians who came upon his cached elk; Jim Deer who took part with him in the battle against the Sioux; Henry Fraeb, "Old Frappe", who died at Battle Mountain from a Cheyenne arrow, "Bigfoot" Davis whom Johnson had met while selling wood to the steamboats plying the river; "Apache Joe" (José Millardo) who was killed by the Apaches; Big Anton, bent on exterminating the Apaches for killing his compadre, Apache Joe; Old John "Portuguese" Phillips, who was the only one to volunteer to ride out to get help for Fort Kearny to save the garrison from Red Cloud and his warriors, and "X" Beidler and "Pack-Saddle" Ben Greenough, who related stories of John Johnson.

George Grinnell saw John Johnson eat an Indian's liver and exclaimed, "Now I see how "Liver-Eating" Johnson got his name!" This name was nearly a life-long nickname.

Poncho Robles, whose riata (lasso) once snatched a knife thrown by Big Anton Sepulveda into a coin on a tree, observed by others. Those watching may have included Mariano Modeno, who honed his knife on the boot of Big Anton, Arkansas Pete Arnold, Hatchet Jack Ireland, Mad Mose and Wild Ben. An unusual trait of Arkansas Pete was that he wore heavy cavalry boots, both winter and summer. Nearly every one of the other mountain men wore moccasins.

Del Gue called Old Mizzou a "master trapper". A little later on, when Johnson and Del spent a few weeks resting in Leadville, they met up with Texas Jack Omohundro and Colorado Charley Utter. Seeing many "tenderfoots" in town, they scurried back to the mountains.

Arkansas Pete, at age 70, was still hunting and trapping in Alberta and invited Johnson to join him up there. It was land the Hudson's Bay Company had trapped much earlier, but there was quite a bit of good trapping again, now that much time had passed. Arkansas Pete was described as having grey hair to his waist, a mustache and beard trimmed with shears, in robust health. He carried a "Mormon Bible" given to him by "Mormon Jack", another trapper and mountain man who'd swiped it from a church. We're told that while neither of the two could read, they had memorized parts that had been read to them and had been marked in their books. Johnson had just retired from being a sheriff.

Why they travelled in groups

After saluting these less-known mountain men, we get back to the story of "Liver-Eating" Johnson.

John became very skilled as a trapper and he was a big and capable man in every respect. He married a young Flathead woman who was very attractive to him as she had not had her head "flattened" the way their tribe customarily did to the babies. She was given the name "The Swan".

It was common for mountain men to take Indian brides

They had not been married very long when he had to head to the big snows for a couple of months of intense trapping, so he laid up food for the animals, built a new corral, chopped wood for the fire, prepared all other needful things and departed.

When he returned, he found that his wife, The Swan, had been killed right in front of the little cabin and their unborn infant, as well. When he had left, they hadn't yet known that she was pregnant. Their bones were already picked clean by vultures. The attackers had stolen or ruined everything but a copper kettle left in the cabin.

Johnson carefully placed all the bones in the copper container and cached it in some rocks. He would return to that same spot every once in a great while, probably to keep his purpose in mind.

Famous vendetta

This deed was done by some young untried braves from the Crow tribe, and they set off a reaction that would punish the whole tribe. It is estimated that, over time, Johnson himself killed upwards of 300 of the Crows. His vendetta became known among trappers and Indians alike.

The Crow tribe even designated a group of 20 warriors who, working individually, set out to be the one to take out John Johnson.
Over a period of 10 to 14 years, Johnson met each one of the designated killers, one at a time, as they came upon him. He killed them all. He seemed to have a sixth sense about when one was around and *always* faced off with each one, never trapping or taking the advantage at first until the warrior knew who he was facing and how he was going to die. His trademark was always a slashed abdomen with the liver removed.
He also scalped his would-be killers.

Only a few trappers ever saw him eat a liver, but it *was* actually observed and recorded. Del Gue, for one, did see this act and it repulsed him. It made him physically sick.

> Eventually, Johnson made peace with the Crow, who became "his brothers", and his personal vendetta against them finally ended after twenty-five years and scores of Crow warriors had fallen. The West, however, was still a very violent and territorial place, particularly during the Plains Indian Wars of the mid-19th century. Many more Indians of different tribes would know the wrath of "Crow Killer" and his fellow mountain men.

Another side of this man

Now, on the other hand, we hear of a very thoughtful and compassionate man. There was a family named Morgan traveling in a wagon train to Oregon. People pretty much always traveled in large groups with a number of wagons and people for protection from Indians and from the elements, and for guides to lead them.

Because of some disagreement or because of simple impatience, John Morgan determined to go it alone and separated his family of a wife, an 18-year-old daughter, and two young sons from the larger group. They rested a few days while everyone else moved on. They repaired a wagon wheel, fished, and grazed the animals.

When the oxen didn't come back one night, John went out to find them. When he didn't return, the sons went to look for him. Still later, the daughter went to look for them all. The mother heard her scream and went running. John Morgan had been tied to a tree and scalped. The sons were both scalped and lying dead and the daughter was stripped, raped and was suffering the last few moments of her life. Blackfoot warriors were all about. The woman went insane, and in her fury somehow managing to kill four of the Blackfeet.

Snowy descent

John Johnson, coming upon this horrible scene, could see what had occurred, even though Mrs. Morgan was incapable of communicating. He helped her bury her three dead children and dug a fourth grave for her husband's scalp. From then on, Johnson left food and goods on her doorstep, somewhat regularly. If he killed an elk or deer, he left a package of fresh meat on her doorstep. If he gained supplies, some ended up at her cabin. Several others may have come to do this, as well.

Mrs. Morgan survived for many years until one harsh winter, when no one could go out, Mrs. John Morgan - Crazy Woman - starved to death. She was found later. The Crows, out of respect for Liver-Eating Johnson, their enemy and her friend, had buried Crazy Woman, and this act helped Johnson to let go of his vendetta against the Crow Tribe. Much later, Old Mose, the trapper, was found to be none other than John Morgan!

Battle between cavalry and Indians, painting by Charles Schreyvogel

It thoroughly angered the mountain men when traders sold guns to the

Indians, in particular repeating guns. Those trappers who came on the scene later saw Indians battle with the army, settlers and homesteaders.

Unfortunately, a lot of lives were lost that did not need to be. These were the times of the treaties, reservations – and broken treaties.

Savior again

Johnson helped and rescued many others, as well. Not far from a fort where she was picking berries, Johnson rescued a white woman from Sioux Indians. The Indians had a chance to scalp her but that is as far as they got. She fainted. Mountain men pursued them, chasing them into a boxed wash, where they massacred them all. The woman, recovered from her brush with death, always afterwards wore a wig over her scarred scalp.

Sharpshooter

Though Johnson's stint in the Union Army was not a long one, he gained a lot of attention as a sharpshooter. Because of his skill with horses, he was first placed in the cavalry, Colorado 2nd, Company H. Although it is a little known fact, Indians did fight on both sides in the Civil War. Johnson took some scalps, which got him a little grief. He told Del Gue about it later.

When he was mustered out, he traded his Union uniform to an Indian for horse and outfit and caught up with Del, who was trapping on Little Medicine Bow in Wyoming. It was along about this time that the 20th Crow warrior sent to kill him showed up and was summarily dispensed with!

Del Gue, White Eye and Pete Coyle were with Johnson at his cabin, which appeared not to have any possibilities for escape, backed up as it was against a high cliff. The men were preparing pelts and telling stories, like the one about Yankee Judd with a gale behind him and a prairie fire in front.

Johnson stepped outside for a moment and came back in to tell the men that Blackfeet had taken their horses and mules. The men were all concerned, but Liver-Eating Johnson just stoked up the fire. He started making biscuits - lots of biscuits.

A rustic cabin of hand-hewn logs

As Johnson worked, the others noticed that he was putting into the mix the strychnine used to bait wolves! The trappers escaped through a cave that only Johnson knew about and, as they departed, they left a lot of biscuits in plain sight. Sure enough, the Blackfeet returned in daylight and wolfed down the biscuits. Old Jim Baker and Arapaho Joe came upon the sight in the spring and counted 29 still figures sitting up against the cliff!

In Leadville, Colorado, the times were changing too, and there were outlaws, crooks, prostitutes, and other riffraff, as well as the honest law-abiding folk. A couple of troublesome miners started to shove Johnson around. He grabbed them and banged their heads together, just as the sheriff appeared. The sheriff started to warn Johnson about knocking people around, and Johnson said, "Keep them off of *me*, then." People in the crowd told the sheriff who he was talking to. The two men ended up shaking hands. Meanwhile, the two miners took off and Johnson accepted a position as deputy.

The mining town of Leadville, Colorado, about 1870

While he was sheriff, old Wind River Jake, another of the mountain men from way back, came to see him in Leadville. He told Johnson that Del Gue wanted him up in the Milk River country at Arkansas Pete's place.

Since Johnson had cleaned up Leadville anyhow, he sent in his resignation and headed out. When he got there, he found Pete had been killed by an Assiniboine warrior. Johnson trailed the warrior and killed him with his bare fists.

Assiniboine man, Pigeon's Egg Head, painting by George Catlin, Smithsonian Museum

"Keep your scalp!"

Johnson trapped with Del Gue into the late 80's. When they parted, like all mountain men, they took their leave with casual words, "Keep your scalp!" - or some other affectionate, but tough, remark.

In 1888, Johnson was still trapping while serving as sheriff in Red Lodge, Montana. His health failed in 1895 and he went to California to the Veterans' Hospital, dying there in January, 1900, just as the new century was beginning.

The inscription over his grave reads: John Johnston, Co. H, 2nd Colorado Cavalry. How much more might have been inscribed there.

Liz Sartori

Chapter 20

Modern-day Mountain Man Rendezvous

"The Greeting" by Alfred J. Miller; mountain men gathering for rendezvous

Oh, the sights and sounds of the rendezvous - the fry bread and Navajo tacos, the variety and fine quality of mountain man goods, authentic materials and crafts you may get there! The Indian dancers in authentic dress, rhythm, and drums, the reenactments, black powder shoots and contests. The fun of experiencing a historic day, a weekend, a week of your life, walking back in time to an era of independence, adventure, entrepreneurship, courage and tenacity! Y'all come to the rendezvous!

All across the country, rendezvous are underway. In addition to those listed here, California, Iowa, Kansas, Missouri, Nebraska, Ohio, Oklahoma, South Dakota, and Texas also hold rendezvous events. See each individual state for local rendezvous schedules. Choose one or choose several and enjoy an unforgettable taste of the mountain man days.

Activities at a Mountain Man Rendezvous Today

Sales
Arts
Crafts
Leather work
Jewelry
Clothing
Indian fry bread

Events for adults and children
Frying-pan throw for women
Bead decorating for children
Blacksmith forge
Trap setting demonstrations

Competitions
Black-powder shoot
Knife-throw
Tomahawk-throw
Indian dancers
Primitive fire-making

Jenny and Dale "Sasquatch" Cottrell attend a modern-day rendezvous

Blackwater and Davis Creek Muzzleloaders Living History Trade Fair
March 1, 2014
Concordia, Missouri

Annual Southwestern Regional Rendezvous
"Attend the ruckus, the rowdy, the renowned"
March 8-15, 2014
Rocking S Ranch, Lampasas, Texas
Booshway: Josh Kuntz
512-619-9216
jgkuntz2012@gmail.co
Segundo: Taylor Tomlin
361-319-2287

Free Trappers of Illinois Spring Rendezvous
March 14-16, 2014
Camp DuBois, Woods River, Illinois
Neal 618-604-3852
Blair 618-616-3219

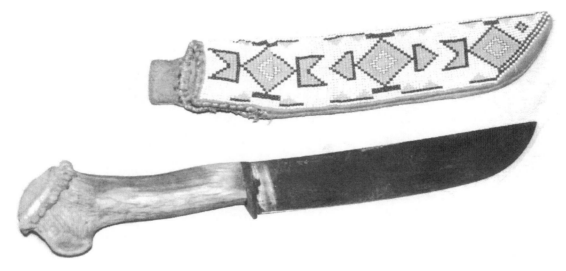

Knife with elk-antler handle and deer-leather beaded sheath, courtesy Dan "Log-Killer" James

Fort Buena Ventura Rendezvous
April 18-20, 2014

Ogden, Utah
Turn off Rt. 15 onto 24th St. exit. Head east to A Ave., then south ½ block to parking lot.
Charles Willis: 801-589-0264
lonewolfhiker@hotmail.com

Anasazi Free -Trapper Spring Rendezvous
April 24-27, 2014, near St. George, Utah
Booshway: Soaring Bird Al Hone
801-367-5560
www.anasazifreetrappers.org

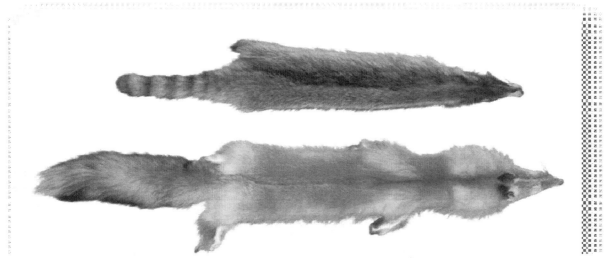

Coon pelt; fox pelt, courtesy Al Loris

Bitteroot Rocky Mountain Rendezvous
Late April - Early May, 2014
Eureka, Montana
randy@welcome2eureka.com

Uncompahgre Free-trapper Happy Canyon Primitive Rendezvous
May 22-26, 2014

Montrose, Colorado
woodman@rockymountains.net
719-539-4460
Conagher@rendezvous-country.com

Cache Valley Rendezvous
May 23-May 26
Hyrum, Utah, just south of Logan
Turn off to Hardware Ranch
Blacksmith's Fork Canyon
Website: explorelogan.com

Lancaster's Restoration Rendezvous
May 23-26, 2014
Fort Lupton, Colorado
Booshway: John Keeling
303-594-6201

Knife hand-crafted from a bear jaw, courtesy Dale "Sasquatch" Cottrell

Port-Neuf Mountain Man Rendezvous
May-June 2014
McCammon, Idaho

I-15, Exit 44
bsnorider@msn.com

1838 Rendezvous
July 2-5, 2014
Riverton, Wyoming
Booshway: Rick "Smokinghawk" Lechner
rlechner49@gmail.com
307-349-4327
1838 Rendezvous Association
P.O. Box 1838
Riverton, WY 82501
"Pre-1840 dress strictly enforced."

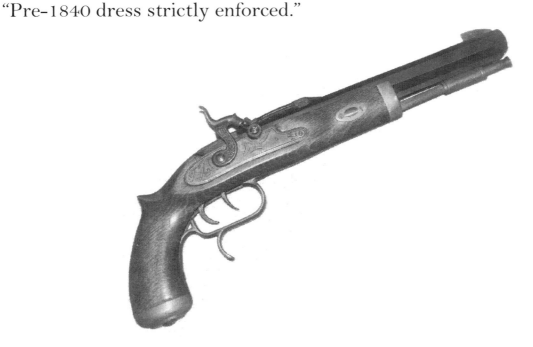

"Patriot" 50-caliber pistol, courtesy Dan "Log-Killer" James

Green River Rendezvous
July 10-13, 2014
Pinedale, Wyoming
Contacts: www.sublettechamber.com
307-367-2242

Rocky Mountain National Rendezvous
July 12-20, 2014
Gunnison, Colorado
http://www.rmnr.org/rendezvous%202014.html

Red Lodge Mountain Man Rendezvous
Late July - early August 2014
Red Lodge, Montana
5.2 miles north of Red Lodge along Hwy 212
Authentic dress required

Smoking Waters Mountain Man Rendezvous and Living History Encampment
Aug. 1-10, 2014
West Yellowstone, Montana
406-646-7931
dmawestyell@omsds.com

Upper Rio Grande Rendezvous
Aug. 2-9, 2014
Creede, Colorado
Booshway: Michelle Hoffman
719-783-0332
Ramona Weber
719-588-9541

Teton Valley Mountain Man Rendezvous
Mid-August
Victor City, Idaho at 9000 S. Hwy. 33
Fur-trade era dress
Contact: City of Victor
208-787-2940

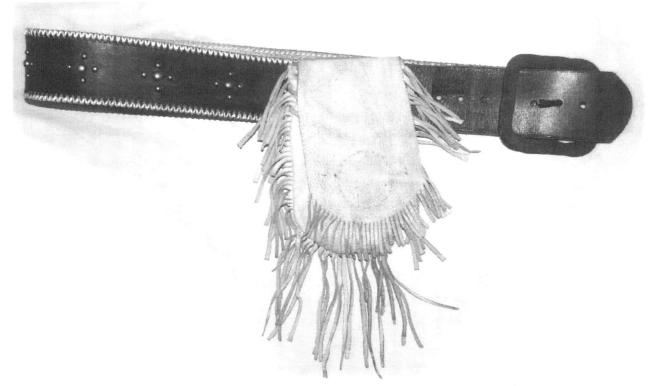

Leather belt with possibles bag, courtesy Dan "Log-Killer" James

Fort Bridger Rendezvous
August 29-Sept. 1
Fort Bridger, Wyoming
Admission $4
In period dress - free admission.
Booshway: Susie Bridge
307-780-8582
susanbridge2@hotmail.com
Segundo: Shalayne Hunziker
801-361-8036
shalaynehunziker@gamil.com

Bell's Fort Free-Trappers and Muzzleloaders Rendezvous
August 13-17, 2014
Westcliffe, Colorado
Booshway: Joe Cace
719-251-8715
Segundo: (Cricket) Dan Hoffman
719-783-0332

Fort Nez Perces

Bear Lake Mountain Man Rendezvous
Aug. 21-25
Laketown, Utah
Contact: Kash Johnson
801-452-1518
kashjohnson1@gmail.com

Interior of Fort Laramie

Liz Sartori

ABOUT THE AUTHOR

Liz Sartori loves to research stories and events from history, especially the history of the United States and its people. The time of the exploration and adventures of the American West is a favorite.

Liz has a Master's Degree in Education and loved to teach her fourth grade students about the mountain men in Utah's history.

She also has the equivalent of half of a master's degree in archaeology and anthropology, and loves studying the American Indians and their cultures. For two years, Liz "dug up the past" of the Ancient Ones in the American Southwest. In her wide-ranging travels, she has enjoyed Indian dancing at the Chippewa Pow-wow in northern Minnesota, the seasonal celebrations of the Hopi in Utah and the Indian dancing at the Fort Bridger Rendezvous in Wyoming.

OTHER BOOKS BY THE AUTHOR

How about a crossword puzzle book about mountain men? Get your companion book entitled *Crossword Puzzles for Mountain Men A to Z*. Have fun!

If you are a crossword puzzle lover or know someone who is, check out the other books in the Crossword Puzzles A to Z series:

Crossword Puzzles for Cat Lovers A to Z

Crossword Puzzles for Country Music Lovers A to Z

Crossword Puzzles for Dog Lovers A to Z

Crossword Puzzles about the Mountain Men A to Z

Crossword Puzzles for Sports Lovers A to Z

If you have ideas for new crossword puzzle books in this series, please contact the author at wildrose.enterprises@gmail.com and share your suggestions. We love to hear from our readers.

Printed in Great Britain
by Amazon.co.uk, Ltd.,
Marston Gate.